دِيـنُ الحَــقّ

THE RELIGION
OF TRUTH

مكتبــــــــة دارالســـــــلام

MAKTABA DAR-US-SALAM

Publishers and Distributors

P.O. Box 21441, Riyadh 11475   ص . ب . ٢١٤٤١ – الريـاض ١١٤٧٥
Tel. 4033962 - Fax: 4021659   ت : ٤٠٣٣٩٦٢ فاكـس : ٤٠٢١٦٥٩
Kingdom of Saudi Arabia   المملـكة العـربيــة السعـوديـة

First Edition   الـطبـعــة الأولى
Supervised by:

ABDUL MALIK MUJAHID

ALL RIGHTS RESERVED   جمـيع حقــوق الطبـع محـفـوظـة

No part of this book may be reproduced or utilized in any form
or by any means, electronic or mechanical, including
photocopying and recording or by any information storage and
retrieval system, without written permission of the publisher.

(هذا الكتاب من منشورات وزارة الشؤون الإسلامية و الأوقاف و الدعوة و الإرشاد) و قد
قامت بطبعه الطبعة مكتبة دارالسلام بإذن من قبل الوزارة برقم (١٣٨/ط) و تاريخ ٢٧/١/١/١٤١٦هـ

Ⓒ

Maktaba Dar-us-Salam , 1994
King Fahad National library Cataloging-in- Publication Data
Al- Omar, Abdul-Rahman bin Hammad
   The Religion of Truth
210 om 1   1161/ 94
... P , .. cm
ISBN: 9960 - 740 -14 - 5
1 - Islam   2 - الاسلام - 1: Title

Legal Deposit No - 1161/94
ISBN: 9960 - 740 - 14 - 5

Printed in 1996 / ١٤١٦هـ

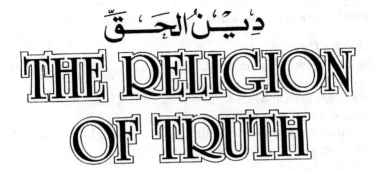

THE RELIGION OF TRUTH

دِيْنُ الحَقِّ

BY

فضيلة الشيخ/عبدالرحمن بن حماد آل عمر

ABDUR RAHMAN BIN HAMMAD AL-OMAR

Maktaba Dar-us-Salam

Publishers and Distributors

Saudi Arabia • USA • UK • Pakistan

Contents

Publisher's Note

We take great pleasure in presenting the readers this book which is of utmost importance towards knowing our Lord, understanding our religion and obeying our Prophet صلى الله عليه وسلم,

This book is written by our brother, Abdur Rahman bin Hammad Al-Omar and provides basic knowledge about the Religion of Truth — Islam, which is a salvation for us not only in this life but also in the Hereafter, the everlasting life.

Because of its importance, this book had been printed, published and widely distributed by the Presidency of Islamic Researches, Ifta and Propagation, Kingdom of Saudi Arabia. We are presenting the revised edition of this book to make it more useful for the readers by selecting the English translation of Qur'ânic verses from the Noble Qur'ân translated by Dr. Muhammad Muhsin Khan and Dr. Muhammad Taqiuddin Hilâli. Another improvement is the presentation of Qur'ânic verses in the Arabic calligraphy of *Mushaf Al-Madinah An-Nabawiya,* which has been printed by the *Mujamma'* of King Fahd of Saudi Arabia for the printing of *Al-Mushaf Ash-Sharif.*

We hope that readers will appreciate our efforts in this regard and get benefited from the book.

Abdul Malik Mujahid
General Manager

In the Name of Allah, the Most Beneficent, the Most Merciful

Preface

All praise be to Allah, the Lord of the worlds. May the peace and blessings be upon Muhammad, the last of the Messengers.

To proceed to my topic, I say:

The Supreme Head Office for Religious Researches, Ifta, Call, and Guidance Departments in the Kingdom of Saudi Arabia gave its approval on the 23rd of Safar 1395 H for the publication of this book, after it had been revised by the competent authorities according to the legal rules of Islâmic Law. I pray to Allah that He may make this book of use to a large number of people.

Abdur Rahman bin Hammad Al-Omar

Introduction and Dedication

All praise be to Allah, Lord of the worlds. May the peace and blessings be upon all of His Messengers.

This is a call for salvation which I would like to present to every wise person, hoping that Allah, the All-Omnipotent and the All-Sublime, would guide by it those who have gone astray, and that He may reward me bountifully and reward everyone who participates in distributing it.

We should know that the only way for our salvation in this life and in the Hereafter is to know, for sure, our Lord who created us, believe in Him, and worship Him Alone. We should also know our Prophet whom Allah had sent to us and to mankind, believe in him and follow him. We should know the religion of truth which our lord has commanded us to believe in, and practise it.

This book...The Religion of Truth, treats these basic and great subjects. I have indicated in the footnotes the meaning of some words and the explanation of some subjects, basing these explanations on The Noble Qur'ân and the *Sunna* (*Ahâdith* — traditions) of Prophet Muhammad صلى الله عليه وسلم , because these two are the only sources of Islâm, the religion of truth. In this book, not only have I dropped blind imitation, which has already misled a large number of people before, but I have also discussed about quite a number of deviated sects which still pretend to be on the right path, although they have gone far astray.

This is an attempt to guide those, who are related to such sects uncautiously, by showing them that these sects have deviated from the path of truth, and to warn others to take precautions for themselves.

May Allah guide me! He is the Most Exalted and on Him I depend.

Chapter One

How to Know Allah,[1] the Great Creator

We should know that our Lord who created us out of naught and sustained us with His bounties is Allah, the Lord of the worlds. The wise believers in Allah did not see Him, but they knew Him by clear evidences showing His Existence and proving that He is the Creator and Sustainer of all creatures.

Some of these evidences are:-

1. The universe, mankind and life are all created objects, with a limited scope of existence. Every incidental and dependent object is created, and thus, must have a creator. This Great Creator is Allah, Who informed us through the Books which He revealed to His Messengers that He is the Originator and the Sustainer of all creatures. The role of His Messengers was to convey Allah's Words to mankind and call people to believe in Allah and worship Him Alone. Allah stated in the Qur'ân:

﴿ إِنَّ رَبَّكُمُ اللَّهُ الَّذِى خَلَقَ السَّمَوَتِ وَالْأَرْضَ فِى سِتَّةِ أَيَّامٍ ثُمَّ اسْتَوَىٰ عَلَى الْعَرْشِ يُغْشِى الَّيْلَ النَّهَارَ يَطْلُبُهُ حَثِيثًا وَالشَّمْسَ وَالْقَمَرَ وَالنُّجُومَ مُسَخَّرَاتٍ بِأَمْرِهِ أَلَا لَهُ الْخَلْقُ وَالْأَمْرُ تَبَارَكَ اللَّهُ رَبُّ الْعَلَمِينَ ﴾

---

[1] Allah is a proper name for the Lord of the world, mankind and every thing. Allah تعالى called Himself by this name which means "The True God".

"Indeed your Lord is Allah, Who created the heavens and the earth in Six Days and then He *Istawa*[1] (rose over) the Throne (really in a manner that suits His Majesty). He covers the night with the day, seeking it rapidly, and (He created) the sun, the moon, the stars subjected to His Command. Surely, His is the Creation and Commandment. Blessed be Allah, the Lord of the *'Alamîn* (mankind, jinns and all that exists)"! (V.7:54)

Through this verse Allah informs mankind that He is their Lord, Who created them, the earth and heavens in six days[2] and that He has firmly established Himself upon His Throne. The Throne is elevated over the heavens. It is the most colossal and greatest thing that Allah had created.

---

[1] *Istawa* is an Arabic word which means "Sat upon, established Himself on". These are the linguistic meanings of the word but, in this verse is the description by which Allah جل has described this action. According to the *Salafi* correct doctrine, no interpretation is permissible for the Attributes and actions of Allah, so, we should restrict ourselves to this word and say that the meaning of *Istawa* in this verse is as Glorious and Majestic to be proper to Allah, Lord of all creation, "Naught is as His likeness, and He is the Omniscient, the Omnipotent." In addition to the above-mentioned, a Muslim shouldn't ask about the way how Allah sat upon His Throne, because the way that Allah sat upon His Throne differs totally from that of His creatures. To explain this *Istiwa,* Imam Ahmed said:- *Istiwa* or sitting upon His Throne is known, but the condition is unknown; to believe therein is a duty or an obligation and to question 'How?' is an innovation — *Bid'a*. This means that nobody knows the condition or the state of how Allah sat upon His Throne save He Himself, Glory be to Him. Speaking about Allah's Attributes is as such speaking about His Identity which is beyond human realisation of Allah's Existence.

[2] Allah is Able to create the whole world in a moment less than a twinkling of an eye. He stated that when He wills to create a thing He says, "Be!" — and it is. The graduation in the creation of the world, in six days, is for a sagacious reason intended by Allah جل.

11

He, Glory be to Him, encompasses all His creatures by His Knowledge and Will. None of their affairs is hidden from Him. Allah also stated that He makes the day to cover the night which follows it in haste, and He created the sun, the moon, and the stars and made them subservient and revolving in their orbits by His Command. Allah informs us that to Him Alone belongs the creation and sovereignty and that He is the Supreme, Transcendent and All-Perfect in Himself and His Attributes, greatly Bountiful, and that He is the Lord of the worlds, who created mankind out of naught, and sustains them with His Bounties.

Allah states in the Qur'ân:-

﴿ وَمِنْ ءَايَٰتِهِ ٱلَّيْلُ وَٱلنَّهَارُ وَٱلشَّمْسُ وَٱلْقَمَرُ لَا تَسْجُدُوا۟ لِلشَّمْسِ وَلَا لِلْقَمَرِ وَٱسْجُدُوا۟ لِلَّهِ ٱلَّذِى خَلَقَهُنَّ إِن كُنتُمْ إِيَّاهُ تَعْبُدُونَ ﴾

"And from among His signs are the night and the day, and the sun and the moon. Prostrate not to the sun nor to the moon, but prostrate to Allah Who created them, if you (really) worship Him." (V.41:37)

In this verse Allah informs us that the day, the night, the sun and the moon are some of His signs. Allah interdicts people from prostrating to the sun or to the moon as they are created objects like other creatures. Allah Alone should be worshipped. Since prostration is a kind of worship, thus, it should be for Allah Alone, because He is the Creator, the Sustainer and the Only True God Who deserves to be worshipped.

2. The creation of male and female.

12

3. The variety of tongues and hues in mankind. Two persons are never identical in colour, voice.... etc. On the contrary, they are quite distinct from each other in one or more of their features or characteristics.

4. Differences of fortunes in life is an evidence of the existence of Allah, the Creator. Although all men are endowed with intellect, knowledge and incentives of competition among each other to gain wealth, acquire dignity or enjoy the favour of having a beautiful wife, they are clearly different in their fortunes. No one has a portion more than that which Allah has assigned to him. The underlying reason for such divergence in fortunes is that Allah tests people, and makes them help and serve each other for the benefit of the whole mankind. Whosoever is unfortunate in this life, but persists believing firmly in Allah, will be rewarded in the Hereafter, and his portion of bliss will be increased in the Gardens. Yet, poor people, even in this worldly life, are endowed generally with a great number of psychological and health privileges of which quite a number of the rich are deprived.

5. Sleep.

6. The soul whose nature is unknown to anyone except Allah.

7. The creation of the human being, his senses, his nervous system, his intellect, and digestive system, ... etc.

8. The rain which Allah sends down to revive the dead earth and brings forth plants of every kind and trees different in kind, colour and taste....... etc. There are only a few of the hundreds of pieces of evidence which Allah the Almighty presented in the Qur'ân. All these evidences prove that Allah is the Living, the Creator and the Sustainer of all creatures.

9. People, by their natural and innate character, believe that they came to existence by the creation and sustenance of a Creator. Allah is the Creator and Sustainer of all creatures. Whoever denies this innate nature is going astray and throwing himself into distress. Thus, the communist, who denies the existence of his Creator and Sustainer, leads a miserable life, and in the Hereafter his end will be in Hell-fire.[1]

Allah تعالى has many attributes. He is the First with no beginning for His Existence. He is Omniscient, Everlasting, Alive; neither He dies, nor does His Existence expire.

He is the Absolute and All-Independent; He is the One with no partners. Allah stated in the Qur'ân:

$$ \text{﴿قُلْ هُوَ ٱللَّهُ أَحَدٌ ٥ ٱللَّهُ ٱلصَّمَدُ ٥ لَمْ يَلِدْ وَلَمْ يُولَدْ ٥ وَلَمْ يَكُن لَّهُ كُفُوًا أَحَدٌ﴾} $$

"Say (O Muhammad صلى الله عليه وسلم): He is Allah, (the) One. *Allah-us-Samad* (السيد الذى يصمد اليه فى الحاجات) (The Self-Sufficient Master, Whom all creatures need, He neither eats nor drinks). He begets not, nor was He begotten. And there is none co-equal or comparable unto Him." (V.112:1-4)

When the disbelievers asked Prophet Muhammad صلى الله عليه وسلم about the Attributes of Allah, Allah revealed this *Sûrah* (chapter) to His Prophet and commanded him to tell them that Allah is One with no partner, The Omniscient, Eternal, Alive and the Sustainer. To Him belongs the

---

[1] Except for he who repents and returns to Allah, believes in Him, His Messenger; His religion, and behaves sincerely according to this belief. Allah accepts the repentance of those who return to Him.

14

Absolute Mastery over the creation, mankind and everything. To Him Alone should people make for refuge and from Him Alone should they ask for help and need. He begets not nor is He begotten; He has no daughter, son, father or a mother; because progeny, birth, and descendant chains are characteristics of creatures and not an Attribute of the Great Creator. In this verse, and other verses of the Qur'ân, Allah negated absolutely the false sayings of Christians who pretend that the Christ is the son of Allah, the false claim of the Jews that Ezra ('Uzair عليه السلام) is the son of Allah and the false belief of others who say that the angels are the daughters of Allah. All these forms of falsehood had been refuted in the Qur'ân; Allah affirmed that He created by His power Jesus Christ ('Iesa عليه السلام) from a mother and without a father, exactly as He had created Adam, the father of mankind out of clay; Eve (Hawwa), the mother of mankind, out of Adam's ribs and their offspring out of their seminal fluids.

Allah created everything; then He decreed a system for His creatures which no one except Him can ever change. Therefore, it is one of the signs of Allah that He created Jesus ('Iesa عليه السلام) from a mother without a father; also the sign of Allah is that He gave Jesus the ability to speak while he was still a baby in the cradle. Allah gave Moses (Musa عليه السلام) the miracle of the staff. This staff turned into a serpent when Moses (Mûsa عليه السلام) cast it, and when he struck the sea with this staff, the sea divided and became a path through which Moses (Mûsa عليه السلام) and his followers were delivered. Allah also gave the Seal of the Prophets, Muhammad صلى الله عليه وسلم , the miracle of the splitting of the moon, made the trees to greet him when he passed by them, and the animals to testify loudly that he is the Messenger of Allah.

Allah carried his Prophet on the *Buraq* from the Sacred Mosque in Makka to the Aqsa Mosque in Jerusalem, then he has been ascended to the heavens accompanied by the angel Gabriel (Jibrael) and have the honour of being in the presence of Allah. Allah تعالى spoke to His Prophet and commanded him and his followers to perform the prayer; on his way back to Makka, the Prophet صلى الله عليه وسلم saw the inhabitants of each heaven, all of these events took place before dawn. The miracle of the journey by night and ascension to the heavens is well-known, it is mentioned in the Qur'ân, Prophetic traditions and history books.

Some of Allah's Attributes: He is the Omniscient, the Omnipotent and has the Ability to do everything; nothing can veil His Seeing or Hearing. Allah knows what is hidden in the wombs, what is concealed in the hearts and knows whatsoever happened and whatsoever will happen. When He desires a thing, He commands "Be!" — and it is. Allah attributed to Himself speech. He speaks to whom He wishes and decrees whatever He wishes. Allah had spoken to Moses (Mûsa عليه السلام) before, and to Muhammad صلى الله عليه وسلم the last of Messengers. The Qur'ân, in its letters and meanings, is the speech of Allah, revealed to His Messenger Muhammad صلى الله عليه وسلم. Therefore, the Qur'ân is one of the Attributes of Allah and not a creation as the erroneous *Mu'tazila* believe. Among the Attributes of Allah by which His Messengers described Him are: His Countenance, His Highness, His pleasure, His wrath .... etc. Allah bestows His pleasure on His believing bondsmen and inflicts His wrath on the disbelievers of his creatures, Allah's Attributes are as Supreme and Majestic as to be proper to Him, Glory be to Allah.

The Qur'ân and Prophetic traditions confirm that the believers will see Allah in the Hereafter while they will be in their eternal abode in Paradise. The Attributes of Allah تعالى have been explained clearly in the Glorious Qur'ân and Prophetic traditions. Thus, he who wishes to know more about these Divine Attributes can consult these sources.

The Raison D'etre
for the creation of Mankind, Jinns and Others

If we know that Allah is our Lord who created us, we should also know that He did not create us without purpose, but to worship Him. The evidence proving this fact is stated in the Qur'ân:

﴿ وَمَا خَلَقْتُ ٱلْجِنَّ وَٱلْإِنسَ إِلَّا لِيَعْبُدُونِ ٠ مَآ أُرِيدُ مِنْهُم مِّن رِّزْقٍ وَمَآ أُرِيدُ أَن يُطْعِمُونِ ٠ إِنَّ ٱللَّهَ هُوَ ٱلرَّزَّاقُ ذُو ٱلْقُوَّةِ ٱلْمَتِينُ ﴾

"And I (Allah) created not the jinns and men except they should worship Me (Alone). I seek not any provision from them (i.e. provision for themselves or My creatures) nor do I ask that they should feed Me (i.e. feed themselves or My creatures). Verily, Allah is the All-Provider, Owner of Power — the Most Strong." (V.51:56-58)

In these verses, Allah stated that He had created the jinns and mankind to worship Him Alone, and that He is All-Independent and not in need of any provision or food from His bondsmen (to Him or to His slaves). Allah is All-Powerful and He is the Donor of livelihood Who sustains mankind and all creatures with His bounties. Allah causes rain to pour down on the earth, and thereby produce all kinds of fruits and bounties with which He favours mankind.

17

As for other creatures which are not endowed with reason, Allah stated that He had created them for the benefit of man. Therefore, man's action and behaviour towards these creatures should be regulated by the Laws of Allah. Every creature, every state of motion or quiescence has been created for a special reason. Allah has stated a lot of these underlying reasons in the Qur'ân; the scholars of Islâmic Law have a good knowledge about this subject, although they differ in rank according to their different levels of knowledge in this field.

Differences in lifetime, means of livelihood, life incidents and even misfortunes of life are caused by the Will of Allah to test His reasonable bondsmen. So, whosoever surrenders to Allah, is contented with what He has for him and endeavours to gain His pleasure, will be rewarded bountifully; Allah will bestow upon him happiness in this life and in the Hereafter. But, whosoever refuses to submit to Allah, is discontented with what He has destined for him and disobeys Him, will suffer the wrath of Allah, and feel misery in this life and in the Hereafter.

May Allah bestow upon us His pleasure and protect us from His wrath.

Resurrection, Day of Judgement, Retribution, Paradise and Hell

If we already know that Allah created us to worship Him, we should also know that Allah had stated in His Scriptures that He will resurrect us after death in order to recompense us for our deeds in this life.

By death, the human being passes from this temporary life to the life of retribution and eternity. When a man's lifetime terminates, Allah orders the angel of death to put an end to his life.

Thus man suffers pains of death when his soul is taken out of his body. Had the man believed in Allah and obeyed Him, his soul will enjoy the abode of bliss (Paradise), but if a man is a disbeliever in Allah, who denies resurrection and retribution after death, his soul will suffer torment till the end of this worldly life when everything in this world will perish; and none will exist save Allah.

Doomsday will begin, and Allah will resurrect all the creation. Everybody will be restored to its soul in the same form as it had been before; even the animals will be raised up again. Then, everyone will be retributed for his deeds, no difference between male and female, head or subordinate, rich or poor. No one will be wronged; every one will have the just reward for his deeds. Whosoever commits injustice, even against animals, will be retributed. As for animals, they will not be questioned because they have no reason, and on that day all animals will be transferred to dust.

Human beings and jinns will be recompensed for their deeds; each one will have his share of reward or punishment according to what he had forwarded during his worldly life. Believers who obeyed Allah and followed His Messengers will be guided to the Gardens, even if they were the poorest men; the disbelievers who denied faith will be led to Hell-fire, even if they were the most noble and rich men in this worldly life. Allah stated in the Qur'ân:

$$﴿ إِنَّ أَكْرَمَكُمْ عِندَ ٱللَّهِ أَتْقَىٰكُمْ ﴾$$

"...Verily, the most honourable of you with Allah is that (believer) who has *At-Taqwa* [i.e. one of the *Muttaqûn*: i.e. pious and righteous persons who fear

19

Allah much (abstain from all kinds of sins and evil deeds which He has forbidden), and love Allah much (perform all kinds of good deeds which He has ordained)]." (V.49:13)

The Garden

The Garden is the abode of bliss; it is beyond description. It has 100 levels; each one of its dwellers will stay in the level suitable to his grade in belief and his obedience to Allah. The lowest grade in the Garden is better by 70 folds than all the worldly blessings which a most luxurious king may ever enjoy.

Hell-fire

May Allah protect us from it. Hell-fire is the abode of torment in the Hereafter. It contains terrible kinds of torment and torture. Had death been possible in the Hereafter, people would have died as soon as they see Hell-fire; but death occurs only once, when the human being passes from this worldly life to the other coming life, and there is no death in the Hereafter, even for the dwellers of Hell-fire.

As I have stated before, a full description of death, resurrection, retribution, Garden, and the Fire is mentioned in many verses of the Glorious Qur'ân. There is much evidence proving resurrection after death, reckoning and retribution. Allah states in the Glorious Qur'ân:

$$ \text{﴿ مِنْهَا خَلَقْنَٰكُمْ وَفِيهَا نُعِيدُكُمْ وَمِنْهَا نُخْرِجُكُمْ تَارَةً أُخْرَىٰ ﴾} $$

"Thereof (the earth) We created you, and into it We shall return you, and from it We shall bring you out once again." (V.20:55)

20

﴾ وَضَرَبَ لَنَا مَثَلًا وَنَسِيَ خَلْقَهُ قَالَ مَن يُحْيِ ٱلْعِظَٰمَ وَهِيَ رَمِيمٌ ٠

قُلْ يُحْيِيهَا ٱلَّذِىٓ أَنشَأَهَآ أَوَّلَ مَرَّةٍ وَهُوَ بِكُلِّ خَلْقٍ عَلِيمٌ ﴿

"And he puts forth for Us a parable, and forgets his own creation. He says: 'Who will give life to these bones when they have rotted away and became dust?' Say (O Muhammad صلى الله عليه وسلم): 'He will give life to them Who created them for the first time! And He is the All-Knower of every creation!' " (V.36:78,79)

﴾ زَعَمَ ٱلَّذِينَ كَفَرُوٓا۟ أَن لَّن يُبْعَثُوا۟ قُلْ بَلَىٰ وَرَبِّى لَتُبْعَثُنَّ ثُمَّ لَتُنَبَّؤُنَّ بِمَا عَمِلْتُمْ وَذَٰلِكَ عَلَى ٱللَّهِ يَسِيرٌ ﴿

"The disbelievers pretend that they will never be resurrected (for the Account). Say (O Muhammad صلى الله عليه وسلم): Yes! By my Lord, you will certainly be resurrected, then you will be informed of (and recompensed for) what you did, and that is easy for Allah." (V.64:7)

In these verses, Allah تعالى informed mankind that He created them on earth as He had created their father Adam from dust before. He will raise them up from their graves, and bring them to account to retribute them for their deeds.

In the second verse, Allah refutes the false pretexts of the disbeliever who denies resurrection, and finds it strange that rotten bones could be revived again. The verse states to such a disbeliever that Allah, who had created these bones before out of naught is certainly able to recreate them as before. In the third verse, Allah orders His Messenger to swear that Allah will raise the disbelievers up after their death, and that Allah will inform them of what they had done before, then retribute them for their deeds; this matter is so easy for Allah.

It is stated in another Qur'ânic verse that it will be said to those, who denied resurrection, while they suffer torture and torment in the Hell, "Taste the torment of Fire which you had belied before".

Controlling and Recording of Man's Deeds and Sayings

Allah تعالى stated that He knows whatsoever any man will do or say, whether it is good or evil, whether it is done openly or in secrecy. All that will happen has been dictated by Allah in the Preserved Tablet even before the heavens, mankind, earth, and other creatures were created.

According to the Qur'ânic verses, every human being is guarded by two angels, one on his right side registering his good deeds, the second on his left side recording whatever evils he commits, and both angels never neglect or miss to register any word or deed. On the Day of Judgement, everyone will receive his own book, in which all his deeds and sayings had been recorded. He will read and confess of all that he had forwarded during his worldly life. If he denies; his own ears, eyes, hands, legs and skin will testify against him. The Glorious Qur'ân has explained all these subjects clearly and in detail:

﴿ مَّا يَلْفِظُ مِن قَوْلٍ إِلَّا لَدَيْهِ رَقِيبٌ عَتِيدٌ ﴾

"Not a word does he (or she) utter, but there is a watcher by him ready (to record it)." (V.50:18)

﴿ وَإِنَّ عَلَيْكُمْ لَحَافِظِينَ ۝ كِرَامًا كَاتِبِينَ ۝ يَعْلَمُونَ مَا تَفْعَلُونَ ﴾

"But verily, over you (are appointed angels in charge

22

of mankind) to watch you, *Kirâman-Kâtibin* [Honourable (near Allah) — writing down (your deeds)], they know all that you do." (V.82:10-12)

The True Testimony

I testify that there is no god but Allah, I testify that Muhammad صلى الله عليه وسلم is the Messenger of Allah. I testify that Paradise and Hell-fire are true, that the Day of Judgement is certain to come, that Allah will raise up people after their death to reckon and retribute them for their deeds. I testify that whatever has been mentioned by Allah in His Book (the Qur'ân) or through the traditions of His Prophet Muhammad صلى الله عليه وسلم, is true.

May I call everyone to believe in this testimony, declare it openly and behave according to its meaning, because this is the only way for salvation.

Chapter Two

Knowing the Messenger

If we already know that Allah is our Lord who created us, and that He will raise us up after death to recompense us for our deeds, we should also know that Allah had sent a Messenger to us and to mankind, and ordered us to obey and follow him. Allah informed us that the only method to know how to worship Him in the right way is to follow this Messenger, and worship Allah according to the religion revealed to him.

This honourable Messenger, that all mankind should believe in and follow, is Muhammad صلى الله عليه وسلم , the unlettered Prophet, the Seal of Messengers, and the Messenger of Allah to mankind.

Both, Moses (Mûsa) and Jesus ('Iesa) announced the glad tidings of Prophet Muhammad's coming. These tidings were clear in more than 40 verses of the Old Testament and Bible, but the Jews and Christians perverted and changed these books.[1]

---

[1] See the book of Ibn Taimiyah — *Al-Jawâb-us-Sahih liman baddala Din-al-Messiah* (The correct answer to those who perverted the religion revealed to the Christ). See also the book of Ibn Al-Qaiyim — *Hidayat-ul-Hayara* (A guide to the perplexed). See also the book of Ibn Hishâm — *Seerat Ibn Hishâm*. And also "Miracles of Prophethood" in the history book of Ibn Katheer — *Al-Bidaya wan-Nihaya.*

24

This honourable Prophet whom Allah had sent to mankind is Muhammad, the son of Abdullah, the son of Abdul Muttalib, the Hashimi and Qurashi. Muhammad was the most honourable and truthful man in the most honourable clan that ever lived on earth. Muhammad, the descendant of the Prophet Ishmael (Ismâ'il), son of Prophet Abraham (Ibrâhim) was born in Makka in the year 570 A.C. The moment of his birth witnessed many indicative events: people were amazed by the brightness casting light over the world, the idols worshipped by Quraish at Makka were reversed, the *Aywân* (palace) throne of Khosrau, king of Persia was shaken that night and a dozen of its battlements broke down. Even the big fire which the Persians used to worship went out, although it had never done so for 2000 years before.

These were all signs and glad tidings to people that the last of the Prophets had been born on that night, that he would demolish idol worshipping and that he would call Arabs, Persians and Greeks to worship Allah Alone and follow His True Religion. These signs were also a warning to these people that if they refused to follow the last of the Prophets, Allah would give him and his followers victory over pagan Arabs, Persians and Greeks; and that the Prophet would propagate his religion, which is an enlightenment from Allah to mankind.

Allah endowed Muhammad صلى الله عليه وسلم by the following favours which characterised him over all other Prophets:-

First:- Muhammad is the Seal of Prophets and no Prophet will be sent after him.

Second:- His Message is a universal and common message. Allah sent him to all nations and not to a special nation or clan.

As the Message of Muhammad صلى الله عليه وسلم is oriented to all the peoples of the world with no distinction among them, therefore, whosoever follows Muhammad's religion and obeys him, will have salvation and find his path to Paradise; and whosoever disobeys him, will dwell in Hellfire. Even the Jews and the Christians are ordered to follow Muhammad صلى الله عليه وسلم; if they disobey him, they will disbelieve not only Muhammad, but also in Moses, Jesus and all other Prophets. All Prophets who preceded Muhammad صلى الله عليه وسلم announced the glad tidings of his coming, and ordered their nations to follow him. Muhammad's religion, Islâm, is the same religion that had been revealed to previous Prophets, except that Islâm got its absolute perfection during the mission of Muhammad صلى الله عليه وسلم , the Seal of Prophets. Consequently, it is not for anyone to adopt any religion other than Islâm, the perfect and true religion which supersedes all other religions. As for Judaism and Christianity, they have both been changed and perverted. On the other hand, every Muslim following Muhammad صلى الله عليه وسلم is, at the same time, a follower of Moses, Jesus, and other Prophets. Every disbeliever of Islâm is also a disbeliever of Moses, Jesus, and other Prophets even if he pretends to be one of their followers. This explains why many Jewish rabbis and Christian monks hastened to embrace Islâm and to believe in Muhammad صلى الله عليه وسلم.

Historians who wrote Prophet Muhammad's biography estimated that the miracles proving his Prophethood number more than one thousand. Among these miracles was the Seal of Prophethood between his shoulders in the form of warts. One of his miracles was that clouds cast shadows upon him wherever he walked in the hot sun in summer, pebbles glorified Allah as he put his hand over them, trees greeted him when he passed by. Also he told of the unseen events to happen in the coming years, and these events turned out to be true, confirming what the Prophet had said before, was certainly a miracle. The unseen events, about which the Prophet had informed us are recorded in books such as the book *An-Nihayah* of Ibn Katheer, the book entitled *Kitâb Al-Akhbâr-ul-Musha'a fi Ashrât-is-Sa'a,* and the chapters dealing with the signs of Doomsday in books of *Ahâdith* (Prophet's traditions and sayings).

All these miracles are similar to the miracles endowed to other Prophets, but Muhammad صلى الله عليه وسلم was privileged with an immortal miracle which no Prophet before him had ever been endowed with, this immortal miracle is the Glorious Qur'ân, the Word of Allah.

Allah undertook to guard the Qur'ân against all sorts of change or pervertion. There are hundreds of millions of copies of Qur'ân all over the world. All these copies are identically similar. If anyone tries to change a letter in a Qur'ânic word, his action will be revealed. As for the Old Testament and Bible, they are diversified; each copy differs from the other, because the Jews and Christians changed these books and perverted them when Allah had entrusted them to guard it. But for the Qur'ân, Allah promised to guard it by Himself. He said:-

﴿ إِنَّا نَحْنُ نَزَّلْنَا ٱلذِّكْرَ وَإِنَّا لَهُۥ لَحَٰفِظُونَ ﴾

"Verily We: It is We Who have sent down the *Dhikr* (i.e. the Qur'ân) and surely, We will guard it (from corruption)." (V.15:9)

Rational and Qur'ânic Evidences
that the Qur'ân is the Speech of Allah
to His Messenger Muhammad صلى الله عليه وسلم

One of the most demonstrative and logical evidences which prove that the Qur'ân is the revelation of Allah to His Messenger Muhammad صلى الله عليه وسلم is the fact that Allah had challenged the disbelievers of Quraish to produce a book like the Qur'ân. Although the Qur'ân was revealed in their own language, and they were masters of fluency, eloquence, poetry and literature, they failed even to produce one *Sûrah* like it. Allah stated that if all of mankind, supported by jinns, try to produce a book like this Qur'ân, they will never be able to produce the like of it:

﴿ قُل لَّبِنِ ٱجۡتَمَعَتِ ٱلۡإِنسُ وَٱلۡجِنُّ عَلَىٰٓ أَن يَأۡتُواْ بِمِثۡلِ هَٰذَا ٱلۡقُرۡءَانِ لَا يَأۡتُونَ بِمِثۡلِهِۦ وَلَوۡ كَانَ بَعۡضُهُمۡ لِبَعۡضٍ ظَهِيرًا ﴾

"Say: If the mankind and the jinns were together to produce the like of this Qur'ân, they could not produce the like thereof, even if they helped one another." (V.17:88)

Had the Qur'ân been the words of Muhammad صلى الله عليه وسلم, or the production of any other mortal; the disbelievers, with their eloquence and fluency, would have been able to face the challenge and produce a *Sûrah* similar to the Qur'ân. But they failed because, the Qur'ân is the Word of Allah. The superiority of the Qur'ân over mortal speech is as the Sublimity of Allah over all His creatures.

As Allah تعالى has no simile, His Words also are not alike to any mortal words.

As the Word of Allah is communicated to mankind through a messenger (angel Jibra'el) sent from Allah, consequently, Muhammad صلى الله عليه وسلم who communicated the Qur'ân to mankind is a Messenger sent from Allah. This has been stated clearly in the Qur'ân:-

﴿ مَّا كَانَ مُحَمَّدٌ أَبَآ أَحَدٍ مِّن رِّجَالِكُمْ وَلَٰكِن رَّسُولَ ٱللَّهِ وَخَاتَمَ ٱلنَّبِيِّـۧنَّ وَكَانَ ٱللَّهُ بِكُلِّ شَىْءٍ عَلِيمًا ﴾

"Muhammad (صلى الله عليه وسلم) is not the father of any man among you, but he is the Messenger of Allah, and the Last (end) of the Prophets. And Allah is Ever All-Aware of everything." (V.33:40)

Allah also said:

﴿ وَمَآ أَرْسَلْنَٰكَ إِلَّا كَآفَّةً لِّلنَّاسِ بَشِيرًا وَنَذِيرًا وَلَٰكِنَّ أَكْثَرَ ٱلنَّاسِ لَا يَعْلَمُونَ ﴾

"And We have not sent you (O Muhammad صلى الله عليه وسلم) except as a giver of glad tidings and a warner to all mankind, but most of men know not." (V.34:28)

Allah said:

﴿ وَمَآ أَرْسَلْنَٰكَ إِلَّا رَحْمَةً لِّلْعَٰلَمِينَ ﴾

"And We have sent you (O Muhammad صلى الله عليه وسلم) not but as a mercy for the 'Alamîn (mankind, jinns and all that exists)." (V.21:107)

In the first verse, Allah stated that Muhammad صلى الله عليه وسلم is His Messenger to mankind, and that he is the last of His Messengers. Therefore, no Prophet will be sent after Muhammad صلى الله عليه وسلم. Allah also stated that He had chosen Muhammad صلى الله عليه وسلم for this noble mission, because he is the most appropriate and perfect human being to carry it out. In the second verse, Allah stated that He had sent Muhammad (صلى الله عليه وسلم) to the whole of mankind with no distinction between races. Muhammad صلى الله عليه وسلم is sent to the whites and blacks, to Arabs and non-Arabs, ... etc, but most men do not understand the truth. They went astray and became disbelievers when they refused to follow Muhammad صلى الله عليه وسلم.

In the third verse, Allah addresses His Prophet and informs him that he had been sent as a mercy to all beings. The Messenger is the Mercy of Allah which He bestowed upon mankind. Therefore, whoever believes in the Prophet and follows him is accepting the Mercy of Allah and will be rewarded by Paradise, and whoever disbelieves in Muhammad صلى الله عليه وسلم and refuses to follow him is rejecting the Mercy of Allah and deserves severe punishment in Hell-fire.

Chapter Three

How to know the Religion of Truth

If man is aware that Allah is the Lord Who has created and nourished him, and that Allah is the Only True God with no partners associated to Him, thus, He is the Only True God that deserves to be worshipped; and if man knows also that Muhammad is the Messenger of Allah to mankind, he must also know that his faith in Allah and his Prophet Muhammad صلى الله عليه وسلم will not be perfect unless he is acquainted with the religion of Islâm, believes in it, and behaves according to its precepts. This is due to the fact that Islâm is the true religion approved by Allah تعالى for mankind. Allah had commanded all His Messengers, before Muhammad, to follow Islâm, and He sent Muhammad صلى الله عليه وسلم the last of His Prophets, to propagate Islâm, and enjoin people to behave according to its precepts.

What is Islâm?

Muhammad صلى الله عليه وسلم, the last Messenger of Allah to mankind, defined Islâm as follows:

«الإِسْلَامُ أَنْ تَشْهَدَ أَنْ لَا إِلَهَ إِلَّا اللهُ، وَأَنَّ مُحَمَّدًا رَسُوْلُ اللهِ، وتُقِيْمَ الصَّلَاةَ، وَتُؤْتِيَ الزَّكَاةَ، وَتَصُوْمَ رَمَضَانَ، وَتَحُجَّ الْبَيْتَ إِنِ اسْتَطَعْتَ إِلَيْهِ سَبِيْلًا» [مُتَّفَقٌ عَلَيْهِ]

"Islâm is to testify that there is no god but Allah and that Muhammad is His Messenger, to perform

31

prayers, pay the *Zakât* (poor tax), fast the month of Ramadan and do pilgrimage to the Sacred House in Makka if you have the means for that".

Islâm is the universal true religion for mankind. Allah stated in the Glorious Qur'ân that:

$$ ﴿ إِنَّ ٱلدِّينَ عِندَ ٱللَّهِ ٱلْإِسْلَٰمُ ﴾ $$

"Truly, the religion near Allah is Islâm..." (V.3:19)

All Messengers of Allah, even those who had been sent before Muhammad صلى الله عليه وسلم adopted Islâm, manifested it, and behaved according to it. The Qur'ân also states:

$$ ﴿ وَمَن يَبْتَغِ غَيْرَ ٱلْإِسْلَٰمِ دِينًا فَلَن يُقْبَلَ مِنْهُ وَهُوَ فِي ٱلْآخِرَةِ مِنَ ٱلْخَٰسِرِينَ ﴾ $$

"And whoever seeks a religion other than Islâm, it will never be accepted of him, and in the Hereafter he will be one of the losers." (V.3:85)

According to these two Qur'ânic verses, Islâm is the only true religion from Allah and no other religion will be accepted in the Hereafter. Therefore, Muslims alone will gain happiness in the next world. Those who die adopting a religion other than Islâm will be of the losers in the next world and will be tormented in Hell-fire.

This explains why all the Prophets who had been sent before Muhammad صلى الله عليه وسلم declared themselves to be Muslims and surrendered to Allah. They declared that they are free of everyone who rejects Islâm. Thus, a Jew or a Christian, who strives for salvation and wants to gain happiness in the Hereafter, should embrace Islâm and follow Muhammad صلى الله عليه وسلم , the Prophet of Islâm. By embracing Islâm, the Jew or the Christian becomes, at the same time, a true follower of Jesus and Moses عليهم السلام because, as it has been mentioned before, Moses, Jesus, Muhammad and all Messengers of Allah who had been sent before Muhammad صلى الله عليه وسلم, were Muslims and called people to Islâm, the true religion of Allah. Whoever is born after the mission of the last Prophet Muhammad صلى الله عليه وسلم should not call himself a Muslim, unless he believes in Muhammad, the Messenger of Allah, follows him and does what Allah commands and avoids what He prohibits. Allah says in the Qur'ân:

﴿ قُلْ إِن كُنتُمْ تُحِبُّونَ ٱللَّهَ فَٱتَّبِعُونِي يُحْبِبْكُمُ ٱللَّهُ وَيَغْفِرْ لَكُمْ ذُنُوبَكُمْ وَٱللَّهُ غَفُورٌ رَّحِيمٌ ﴾

"Say (O Muhammad صلى الله عليه وسلم to mankind): "If you (really) love Allah then follow me (i.e. accept Islâmic Monotheism, follow the Qur'ân and the *Sunna*), Allah will love you and forgive you your sins. And Allah is Oft-Forgiving, Most Merciful." (V.3:31)

In this verse, Allah orders his Messenger Muhammad صلى الله عليه وسلم to tell those who pretend that they love Allah: "If you love Allah truly, follow me and Allah will love you, Allah will never love you nor will He forgive your sins, unless you believe in His Messenger Muhammad and follow him." Allah had sent Muhammad صلى الله عليه وسلم to propagate Islâm, the comprehensive and tolerant religion to all mankind. Allah stated in the Qur'ân that He gave perfection to Islâm and approved it to be the religion of mankind:

﴿ ٱلْيَوْمَ أَكْمَلْتُ لَكُمْ دِينَكُمْ وَأَتْمَمْتُ عَلَيْكُمْ نِعْمَتِي وَرَضِيتُ لَكُمُ ٱلْإِسْلَٰمَ دِينًا ﴾

33

".... This day, I have perfected your religion for you, completed My Favour upon you, and have chosen for you Islâm as your religion..." (V.5:3)

This Qur'ânic verse was revealed to the Seal of Prophets Muhammad صلى الله عليه وسلم during his last pilgrimage while he was standing on the Mount of Arafat, offering his prayers to Allah and thanking Him for His help and that He had accomplished His favors on His Messenger by the completion of the Qur'ân, and that Islâm had begun to take its course by gaining an ever increasing number of followers.

This verse also indicates that Islâm was revealed to Muhammad صلى الله عليه وسلم in order to call all mankind to it, because it is the perfect, comprehensive and suitable religion for mankind in all ages, all places, and for all nations.

This is due to the fact that Islâm is characterised by knowledge, tolerance, justice and good. It contains a clear, perfect and straight method that guides man in all spheres of life. Islâm is not only a faith, but it also has its own distinguished basis of governing, justice, political system, social affairs, economy and whatever useful knowledge which mankind may need to achieve prosperity in this worldly life and happiness in the coming life (after death).

The Pillars of Islâm

Islâm is based on the following (five principles). No one can claim to be a Muslim unless he believes in these five essential rules and practises them sincerely:

1) To testify that none has the right to be worshipped but Allah, and Muhammad صلى الله عليه وسلم is Allah's Messenger.

34

2) To offer the *Salât* (compulsory congregational prayers) dutifully and perfectly.

3) To pay *Zakât* (i.e. obligatory charity).

4) To observe *Saum* (fasts) during the month of Ramadan.

5) To perform *Hajj* (whenever one is capable of).[1]

To testify that there is no god but Allah and that Muhammad صلى الله عليه وسلم is His Messenger, has a specific meaning which the Muslim should not only know, but also practise sincerely. Whoever utters this testimony (*Shahâdah*) without knowing its meaning, or without binding himself by it in his behaviour will not gain anything from it.

This testimony means that there is none on the earth nor in the heavens deserving to be worshipped save Allah Alone. Allah is the One True God. All other deities, whatever they may be, are false. Therefore, whoever worships any deity besides Allah is a disbeliever and an idolater even if what he worships is a prophet, a saint or a holy man, under the pretext that this deity will be his intercessor to Allah. The disbelievers, against whom Prophet Muhammad صلى الله عليه وسلم carried a continuous fight, had used this false pretext to justify worshipping their prophets and pious men. Seeking to gain the consent of Allah, or asking for His help cannot be achieved by worshipping others than Allah, but it can only be attained by serving Allah Alone,

---

[1] The Messenger صلى الله عليه وسلم said:

"The superstructure of Islâm is raised on five pillars:to testify that there is no god save Allah Alone and that Muhammad is His Messenger, to perform the prayer, to pay the *Zakât*, to fast the month of Ramadan and to do pilgrimage to the Sacred House.

glorifying Him by His Names and Attributes, and by performing the good deeds that He had commanded us to do, such as prayer, fasting, fighting for His Cause, pilgrimage and kind treatment to the parents .... etc.

Worshipping takes different forms, and one of them is supplication which means, to ask for something that no one can ever grant except Allah. The fall of the rain, recovery of a patient, relief from misfortune, asking for salvation from Hell-fire and dwelling in Paradise ... etc, in all these cases and other similar cases, one should ask Allah Alone to grant such blessings.

Whoever asks a mortal being to grant him such things is indeed worshipping this being. Allah ordered His bondsmen to supplicate Him Alone for whatever they may need:-

﴿ وَقَالَ رَبُّكُمُ ٱدْعُونِيٓ أَسْتَجِبْ لَكُمْ إِنَّ ٱلَّذِينَ يَسْتَكْبِرُونَ عَنْ عِبَادَتِى سَيَدْخُلُونَ جَهَنَّمَ دَاخِرِينَ ﴾

"And your Lord said: Invoke Me, [i.e. believe in My Oneness (Islamic Monotheism)] (and ask Me for anything) I will respond to your (invocation). Verily! Those who scorn My worship [i.e. do not invoke Me, and do not believe in My Oneness, (Islamic Monotheism)] they will surely enter Hell in humiliation!" (V.40:60)

Allah instructed us that mortal beings, whom idolaters supplicate, are deprived of power; they can never cause harm or bring any benefit to anyone:

﴿ قُلِ ٱدْعُوا۟ ٱلَّذِينَ زَعَمْتُم مِّن دُونِهِۦ فَلَا يَمْلِكُونَ كَشْفَ ٱلضُّرِّ عَنكُمْ وَلَا تَحْوِيلًا ﴾

"Say (O Muhammad صلى الله عليه وسلم): Call unto those besides Him — whom you pretend (to be gods like angels, Messiah, Ezra etc.). They have neither the power to remove the adversity from you nor even to shift it from you to another person." (V.17:56)

The Qur'ân also states:

﴿ وَأَنَّ ٱلْمَسَٰجِدَ لِلَّهِ فَلَا تَدْعُوا۟ مَعَ ٱللَّهِ أَحَدًا ﴾

"And the mosques are for Allah (Alone), so invoke not anyone along with Allah." (V.72:18)

Offering sacrifices and votive offerings are services which should be consecrated for Allah Alone. Whoever offers a sacrifice or makes a vow for a dead pious man, for a jinn or for anyone other than Allah, is an idolater cursed by Allah. The Qur'ân states:-

﴿ قُلْ إِنَّ صَلَاتِى وَنُسُكِى وَمَحْيَاىَ وَمَمَاتِى لِلَّهِ رَبِّ ٱلْعَٰلَمِينَ ٠ لَا شَرِيكَ لَهُۥ وَبِذَٰلِكَ أُمِرْتُ وَأَنَا۠ أَوَّلُ ٱلْمُسْلِمِينَ ﴾

"Say (O Muhammad صلى الله عليه وسلم): Verily, my prayer, my sacrifice, my living, and my dying are for Allah, the Lord of the 'Alamîn (mankind, jinns and all that exists). He has no partner. And of this I have been commanded, and I am the first of the Muslims." (V.6:162,163)

Prophet Muhammad صلى الله عليه وسلم said:

[مُسْلِمٌ]   «لَعَنَ اللهُ مَنْ ذَبَحَ لِغَيْرِ اللهِ»

"May Allah curse whoever offers a sacrifice to anyone other than Him,"

If a person says: "I vow to offer a sacrifice to this if I pass in the examination, or if I am relieved from a disease..... etc." This kind of vow is certainly a form of idolatry, because vows should be consecrated to Allah Alone and absolutely not to anyone else, other than Allah. The right vow in such cases is to say: "I vow to offer a sacrifice to Allah, or I vow to Allah that I will pay to the poor this sum of money, or will give the needy so-and-so, if I succeed in the examination, or be relieved from the disease."

Calling for help, asking for refuge and invoking for support are also among the forms of divine services. One should not call for help, ask for refuge or seek for support from anyone else, other than Allah. The Noble Qur'ân has stated:

$$ \text{﴿ إِيَّاكَ نَعْبُدُ وَإِيَّاكَ نَسْتَعِينُ ﴾} $$

"You (Alone) we worship, and You (Alone) we ask for help (for each and everything)." (V.1:5)

The Noble Qur'ân also states:

$$ \text{﴿ قُلْ أَعُوذُ بِرَبِّ ٱلْفَلَقِ ○ مِن شَرِّ مَا خَلَقَ ﴾} $$

"Say: I seek refuge with (Allah) the Lord of the day-break, from the evil of what He has created". (V.113:1,2)

Prophet Muhammad صلى الله عليه وسلم said:

$$ \text{« إِنَّهُ لَا يُسْتَغَاثُ بِي وَإِنَّمَا يُسْتَغَاثُ بِاللهِ »} $$

$$ \text{[الطَّبَرَانِيُّ حَدِيثٌ صَحِيحٌ]} $$

"Call me not for help, but call Allah, your Lord."

The Prophet also said:

«إِذَا سَأَلْتَ فَاسْأَلِ اللهَ، وَإِذَا اسْتَعَنْتَ فَاسْتَعِنْ بِاللهِ»

[التِّرْمِذِيُّ حَدِيثٌ صَحِيحٌ]

"If you ask for any thing, ask for it from Allah Alone; if you seek for help, seek it from Allah Alone."

It is permissible for a person to ask for his fellow brother's help or support if the matter for which he asks for help is within the scope of human ability. But if such a matter is beyond the scope of human ability, man must not ask for help from anyone except Allah. In all cases, it is strictly forbidden to ask for help or support from a dead man or an absent person, even if he were a Prophet, a saint or an angel.

As for those who pretend to know the unseen, or claim to foresee what is hidden in the future, they are disbelievers and flagrant liars. Even if what they foretell happens, it only happens by chance. Both Imam Ahmad and Al-Hâkim related that the Prophet had said:

«مَنْ أَتَى كَاهِنًا أَوْ عَرَّافًا فَصَدَّقَهُ بِمَا يَقُوْلُ فَقَدْ كَفَرَ بِمَا أُنْزِلَ عَلَى مُحَمَّدٍ» [اَحْمَدُ، اَلْحَاكِمُ]

"Whoever goes to a sorcerer or a fortuneteller and believes in what he says, disbelieves in what had been revealed to Muhammad صلى الله عليه وسلم."

Trust, submissiveness (*Tawakkul*), and hope (*Raja*) are also among the forms of worshipping. Man should never trust, hope or submit to anyone save Allah. It is regrettable that many of those who belong to Islâm still commit idolatry and invoke others than Allah, i.e. notable men of authority, dead pious men ... etc. They circumambulate the graves of dead pious men invoking them for help or to attend their needs. There is no doubt that this is a form of idolatry and whoever performs such an action is not a Muslim, even if he utters the testimony of Islâm and performs all the fundamental duties of Islâm. Allah stated in the Qur'ân:

﴿ وَلَقَدْ أُوحِىَ إِلَيْكَ وَإِلَى ٱلَّذِينَ مِن قَبْلِكَ لَئِنْ أَشْرَكْتَ لَيَحْبَطَنَّ عَمَلُكَ وَلَتَكُونَنَّ مِنَ ٱلْخَـٰسِرِينَ ﴾

"And indeed it has been revealed to you (O Muhammad صلى الله عليه وسلم), as it was to those (Allah's Messengers) before you: If you join others in worship with Allah, (then) surely (all) your deeds will be in vain, and you will certainly be among the losers." (V.39:65)

The Qur'ân also states:

﴿ إِنَّهُ مَن يُشْرِكْ بِٱللَّهِ فَقَدْ حَرَّمَ ٱللَّهُ عَلَيْهِ ٱلْجَنَّةَ وَمَأْوَىٰهُ ٱلنَّارُ وَمَا لِلظَّـٰلِمِينَ مِنْ أَنصَارٍ ﴾

"... Verily, whosoever sets up partners in worship with Allah, then Allah has forbidden Paradise for him, and the Fire will be his abode. And for the Zâlimûn (polytheists and wrong-doers) there are no helpers." (V.5:72)

Allah commanded His Prophet Muhammad صلى الله عليه وسلم to

40

say to the people:

﴿ قُل إِنَّمَآ أَنَا۠ بَشَرٌ مِّثْلُكُمْ يُوحَىٰٓ إِلَىَّ أَنَّمَآ إِلَٰهُكُمْ إِلَٰهٌ وَٰحِدٌ فَمَن كَانَ يَرْجُواْ لِقَآءَ رَبِّهِۦ فَلْيَعْمَلْ عَمَلًا صَٰلِحًا وَلَا يُشْرِكْ بِعِبَادَةِ رَبِّهِۦٓ أَحَدًۢا ﴾

"Say (O Muhammad صلى الله عليه وسلم): I am only a man like you. It has been inspired to me that your *Ilâh* (God) is One *Ilâh* (God — i.e. Allah). So whoever hopes for the meeting with his Lord, let him work righteousness and associate none as a partner in the worship of his Lord." (V.18:110)

Those foolish men are really deluded by wicked ignorant scientists who have acquaintance in some religious branches, but ignore absolutely the basic principle of Faith, that is *Tauhid* (Oneness of Allah).

Using deviated interpretations, false traditions imputed to the Prophet صلى الله عليه وسلم misled by lust, satanic dreams and all other forms of misguidance, those wicked pretenders call people to believe in the intercession of pious men and thus support idolatry by all means.

Those demons who follow blindly their ancestors and adopt the same behaviour of ancient idolaters are disbelievers and evil-doers.

﴿ وَٱبْتَغُوٓاْ إِلَيْهِ ٱلْوَسِيلَةَ ﴾

"Allah ordered us to seek the means of approach to Him..." (V.5:35)

The means of approach which we are commanded to seek are well-known. They consist of performing righteous deeds, believing in the Oneness of Allah, offering *Salât* (prayer), paying *Zakât*, fasting during the month of

41

Ramadan, performing *Hajj* (pilgrimage) and striving with might and main in the Cause of Allah. Invoking dead men in times of affliction and distress has nothing to do with the means of approach to Allah, it is rather against these means and contrary to the basic faith of Islâm *Tauhîd* or belief in the Oneness of Allah.

It is true that Prophets, pious men and some other Muslims will be endowed with the favor to intercede for others, but they will never have such favor save by the Will of Allah. Intercession is an exclusive Divine prerogative. No one can ever intercede for another except by the Will of Allah. Therefore, a true monotheist never invokes the dead for intercession, because a dead man can never remove harm or bring benefit, in all cases the true Muslim invokes Allah saying: "O Allah, I pray to you to bestow upon me the intercession of Your Prophet and pious men".

Allah says in the Noble Qur'ân:

$$﴿ قُل لِّلَّهِ ٱلشَّفَٰعَةُ جَمِيعًا لَّهُۥ مُلۡكُ ٱلسَّمَٰوَٰتِ وَٱلۡأَرۡضِ ثُمَّ إِلَيۡهِ تُرۡجَعُونَ ﴾$$

"Say: To Allah belongs all intercession. His is the Sovereignty of the heavens and the earth, then to Him you shall be brought back." (V.39:44)

Taking graves as places of worship, kindling lights thereon, constructing buildings over them, plastering, decorating them with curtains, or performing prayers thereon, all these actions are flagrant forms of heresy and are strictly prohibited by the Noble Prophet صلى الله عليه وسلم.

Ignorant people who circumambulate the graves of Al-Badawi and Sayidah Zainab in Egypt, Al-Jilani and the so-called notable descendants of the Prophet in Najaf,

42

Karbala and other cities of 'Irâq, and round other graves elsewhere, commit flagrant idolatry because they believe that these buried bodies have the ability to bring benefits or cause harm to them, and that they could help them attain their needs. Such men are not only lost idolaters, but they are disgraced even if they pretend to be Muslims and do what Muslims do.

To be a true monotheist, it is not enough to utter: "There is no god save Allah and Muhammad is His Messenger", but, it is essential for a Muslim to be aware of the meaning of this testimony and behave accordingly.

For those who embrace Islâm and desist from false creed, it is enough for them to utter first the testimony of Islâm. By doing this they become Muslims as long as they do not behave in a way contrary to the principles and morals of Islâm.

Prophets and pious men, are innocent of the idolatrous deeds of those who invoke them or ask them for help. They are aware of the fact that Allah had sent His Messengers to call people to abandon worshipping any being save Allah, even if they were Prophets or pious men. The way in which a true Muslim can show his love and affection to the Prophets and pious men is to follow their good way, taking them as models in deeds and behaviour. It is a religious duty for every Muslim to love the Prophets and pious men, but he must never worship them. Muslims believe that they not only should love Prophet Muhammad صلى اللـه عليـه وسـلم, but they should also prefer him to their ownselves, kins, sons and all other people.

The Group that will be delivered

Although Muslims are great in number, yet only a few of them are true Muslims. There are 73 Muslim sects with hundreds of millions of followers; however only one of these sects are true Muslims. Those are the ones who follow the way of Prophet Muhammad صلى الله عليه وسلم, and the way of his faithful Companions, both in matters of faith and good behaviour. *Bukhâri* and *Muslim* report that the Prophet صلى الله عليه وسلم said:

«افْتَرَقَتِ الْيَهُوْدُ عَلَى إِحْدَى وَسَبْعِيْنَ فِرْقَةً، وَافْتَرَقَتِ النَّصَارَى عَلَى اثْنَتَيْنِ وَسَبْعِيْنَ فِرْقَةً، وَسَتَفْتَرِقُ هٰذِهِ الأُمَّةُ عَلَى ثَلَاثٍ وَسَبْعِيْنَ فِرْقَةً كُلُّهَا فِي النَّارِ إِلاَّ وَاحِدَةً قَالَ الصَّحَابَةُ: مَنْ هِيَ يَا رَسُوْلَ اللهِ؟ـ قَالَ مَنْ كَانَ عَلَى مِثْلِ مَا أَنا عَلَيْهِ الْيَوْمَ وَأَصْحَابِيْ» [مُتَّفَقٌ عَلَيْهِ]

"The Jews had split into 71 sects, the Christians had dispersed into 72 sects and this nation (the Muslim nation) will disperse into 73 sects; all of them will dwell in Hell-fire, except one." When the Companions asked the Prophet صلى الله عليه وسلم about the group that will be delivered, he said: "It is the group that will follow my way and my Companions' way".

The Prophet صلى الله عليه وسلم and his Companions were quite aware of the meaning of "No God save Allah." Therefore, they stuck to Monothiesm both in faith and behaviour, they invoked none save Allah, offered sacrifices or made vows to none save Allah, supplicated in distress to none save Allah, asked for help only from Allah and believed that none could profit them or hurt them save Allah. The Prophet صلى الله عليه وسلم and his Companions performed sincerely all Islâmic duties for the sake of Allah. They believed in Allah, His Angels, His Books, His Messengers, the Day of Resurrection and Judgement, and in the Divine Decree, the good thereof and the evil thereof. True Muslims consult the Glorious Qur'ân and Prophetic traditions in all affairs of life and accept with the fullest conviction the solutions based on Qur'ânic commandments and Prophetic traditions. Devout Muslims give their intimacy to those who are sincere to the Cause of Allah, and they are foes to the enemies of Allah. They call to Allah, strive in His way, obey their Muslim ruler, enjoin right conduct and forbid indecency and wherever they are, they say nothing but the truth.

Devout Muslims not only show their love and affection for the Prophet صلى الله عليه وسلم , but also to his wives, progeny and Companions. They never discriminate among them, nor do they prefer one of them to the other; they respect them all, each one for his own merits. True Muslims do not busy themselves with the disputes that happened among those noble Companions. They never believe that they committed the offences which some hypocrites attribute to them. They know that the aim of the hypocrites is to disperse the Muslim nation. But it is regrettable that some Muslim scholars and historians were deceived by these false accusations of the hypocrites and registered them in their books.

Those who claim to be the noble descendants of the Prophet صلى الله عليه وسلم should first verify their ancestral line to be sure of their claim. Allah has cursed whoever relates himself to someone other than his father. If what they claim to be is true, they should follow the right way of the Prophet and his noble progeny by being sincere in adoring Allah, desisting from sins, not allowing people to kiss their hands and feet, and finally, they should not distinguish themselves by wearing a special uniform. All these forms of behaviour are contrary to the Prophet's way, and he is innocent of those who adopt a way different from his manner. In fact, according to the Qur'ân, the noblest Muslim near Allah is he who fears Him most. May Allah guide us to the right path, and may His Blessings and Peace be upon our Prophet Muhammad, his progeny and his Companions.

Sovereignty and Legislative Power
are Exclusive Rights of Allah

Sovereignty and legislative power are exclusive Rights of Allah. This is an immediate conclusion of Monotheism. Nobody has the right to enact a law contrary to the Law of Allah. A Muslim should never govern or judge by laws different from the Laws of Allah, nor should he give his consent to any form of judgement or government based on laws contrary to the Laws of Allah. According to the Islâmic faith, no one has the right to forbid what Allah has made legal, nor can he legalize what Allah has forbidden. Whoever commits intentionally such a deed or approves it is a disbeliever. The Noble Qur'ân states that:

﴿ وَمَن لَّمْ يَحْكُم بِمَآ أَنزَلَ ٱللَّهُ فَأُوْلَٰٓئِكَ هُمُ ٱلْكَٰفِرُونَ ﴾

"... And whosoever does not judge by what Allah has revealed, such are the *Kâfirûn* (i.e. disbelievers — of a lesser degree as they do not act on Allah's Laws)." (V.5:44)

The mission of Allah's Prophets is to call people to believe in Monotheism and behave according to its precepts. They try to deliver people from the bonds of man worship to the blessings of Allah's service, and to convince them to submit to the Laws of Allah instead of submitting themselves to man-made laws.

Whoever recites the Glorious Qur'ân attentively and keeps

46

away from following blindly people's opinion, will know that Allah had assigned for man his duties towards Him and his relation with Allah's other creatures.

The servant believing in Allah is aware that all kinds of service should be dedicated to Allah Alone and no partner is to be attributed with Him. He knows also that his duty towards Prophets and pious men is to follow in their footsteps and express his love to them. As for the enemies of Allah, although it is the duty of the believer to detest them because they are detested by Allah, yet the believer is authorized to call them to Islâm and explain its noble meaning to them; they may be guided by such a call and embrace Islâm. But if they reject it and refuse to submit to the Laws of Allah, a Muslim is permitted to fight them until idolatry is uprooted and the Religion of Allah gains victory over polytheism.

The Notion of acknowledgement that Muhammad صلى الله عليه وسلم is the Messenger of Allah

To testify that Muhammad is the Messenger of Allah means to know and believe sincerely that Muhammad صلى الله عليه وسلم is the Prophet and Messenger whom Allah had sent to all peoples of the world. It means also that Muhammad is a servant of Allah, thus he must not be worshipped, because worshipping is due to Allah Alone. As Muhammad صلى الله عليه وسلم is the Messenger of Allah, he must be followed and obeyed, not denied. Whoever obeys Muhammad صلى الله عليه وسلم will abide in the Garden and whoever disobeys him will abide in Hell-fire. Allah says in the Noble Qur'ân:

$$﴿ وَمَآ ءَاتَىٰكُمُ ٱلرَّسُولُ فَخُذُوهُ وَمَا نَهَىٰكُمْ عَنْهُ فَٱنتَهُواْ ﴾$$

"... And whatsoever the Messenger (Muhammad صلى

صلى الله عليه وسلم) gives you, take it, and whatsoever he forbids you, abstain (from it), and fear Allah. Verily, Allah is Severe in punishment." (V.59:7)

﴿ فَلَا وَرَبِّكَ لَا يُؤْمِنُونَ حَتَّىٰ يُحَكِّمُوكَ فِيمَا شَجَرَ بَيْنَهُمْ ثُمَّ لَا يَجِدُوا فِي أَنفُسِهِمْ حَرَجًا مِّمَّا قَضَيْتَ وَيُسَلِّمُوا تَسْلِيمًا ﴾

"But no, by your Lord, they can have no Faith, until they make you (صلى الله عليه وسلم) judge in all disputes between them, and find in themselves no resistance against your decisions, and accept (them) with full submission." (V.4:65)

This means that, according to the Islâmic Faith all acts of devotion, all rules of legislation and government, and all rules that explain what is lawful and what is forbidden, should be nothing else than that which had been conveyed to people by the Noble Messenger of Allah, Muhammad صلى الله عليه وسلم. The Muslim should not believe in any legislation different from what is transmitted by Muhammad صلى الله عليه وسلم, the Messenger of Allah.

These last two Qur'ânic verses mean that Muslims should obey Muhammad صلى الله عليه وسلم, the Messenger of Allah in what he commanded them, and desist from all that he prohibited them, because the Messenger neither commanded nor prohibited according to his own desires, but he used to do this in conformity with the revelations of Allah. It is also reported by *Muslim* that the Prophet صلى الله عليه وسلم said:

«مَنْ عَمِلَ عَمَلًا لَيْسَ عَلَيْهِ أَمْرُنَا فَهُوَ رَدٌّ» [مُسْلِمٌ وَغَيْرُهُ]

"Whoever performs a deed that is not in conformity with our principles, his deed will be rejected."

48

Thus, any wise man who wishes to attain happiness in this present life and in the Hereafter and gain salvation after death, should testify that: "There is no God save Allah, and that Muhammad is His Messenger". He should also behave according to the notion of this testimony and practise the other fundamental principles of Islâm which constitute the proper way to worship Allah.

Salât (Prayer) — The Second Pillar of Islâm

The second pillar of Islâm is *Iqâmat-as-Salât* (performing prayer). The Muslim is enjoined to perform five obligatory prayers every day to keep himself in relation with his Lord, to invoke and implore Him, and to refrain himself from committing lewdness or indecency. These prayers not only ensure mental peace to the Muslim in this present life, but they also pave the way to him to gain eternal happiness in the Hereafter.

To perform prayer, one should be clean, wearing clean clothes and pray in a clean place.

Before prayer, the Muslim should cleanse himself with clean water, removing all traces of stool, urine, or any other dirt. In this way he purifies himself physically and morally.

Prayer is the pillar of religion. It follows in importance the two testimonies. Therefore, it is not only a duty on a Muslim to perform prayers from his maturity up to his death, but he should also order his household to perform it. He should also order his children to start practising it from the time when they are 7 years old so that they may be accustomed to perform it promptly. Evidence from the Qur'ân:

﴿ إِنَّ ٱلصَّلَوٰةَ كَانَتْ عَلَى ٱلْمُؤْمِنِينَ كِتَٰبًا مَّوْقُوتًا ﴾

"... Verily, the prayer is enjoined on the believers at fixed hours." (V.4:103)

Further evidence from the Qur'ân:

﴿ وَمَآ أُمِرُوٓاْ إِلَّا لِيَعۡبُدُواْ ٱللَّهَ مُخۡلِصِينَ لَهُ ٱلدِّينَ حُنَفَآءَ وَيُقِيمُواْ ٱلصَّلَوٰةَ وَيُؤۡتُواْ ٱلزَّكَوٰةَۚ وَذَٰلِكَ دِينُ ٱلۡقَيِّمَةِ ﴾

"And they were commanded not, but that they should worship Allah, and worship none but Him Alone (abstaining from ascribing partners to Him), and offer prayers perfectly (*Iqâmat-as-Salât*) and give *Zakât*: and that is the right religion." (V.98:5)

In the first of these two verses, Allah tells us that prayer is a prescribed duty on all believers and that they should fulfil this duty at its fixed time. In the second verse, Allah makes it well-known to mankind that He had created them in order to worship Him Alone, be sincere in their devotion to Him, perform prayer and pay the *Zakât* (i.e., obligatory charity) to those who deserve it. The Prophet صلى الله عليه وسلم said:

«الْعَهْدُ الَّذِي بَيْنَنَا وَبَيْنَهُمُ الصَّلَاةُ فَمَنْ تَرَكَهَا فَقَدْ كَفَرَ»
[حَدِيثٌ صَحِيحٌ]

"The obligation which distinguishes between us and the disbelievers is prayer, therefore, whoever desists from prayer, becomes a disbeliever."

Thus, prayer is a duty on the Muslim in all circumstances. Even if he is sick or frightened he should perform his daily prayers, sitting, standing or lying. If he is unable to perform them in any of these ways, he is permitted to perform it by his eye-gestures, or even in his heart.

The five obligatory daily prayers are the morning prayer (*Fajr*), the noon prayer (*Zuhr*), the afternoon prayer ('*Asr*), the evening prayer (*Maghrib*) and the night prayer ('*Ishâ*').

The time due for morning prayer begins at true dawn and extends until the sun rises. It should not be delayed beyond this span of time. The time for noon prayer starts from the *Zawâl* (a little after the sun has passed the meridian) and extends till one's shadow becomes equal to his own length plus the length of its noon-time shadow. The time enjoined for afternoon prayer starts after the end of noon-prayer time and extends until the sun turns yellow. One must hasten to perform it while the sun is still bright. The evening prayer time begins soon after sunset and lasts till the disappearance of the twilight. Its performance should not be delayed. The night prayer time begins after the disappearance of the twilight and lasts till midnight. If a Muslim delays one of these five prayers, he commits a grievous sin. He should turn to Allah for repentance and refrain himself from repeating it. The Qur'ân warns those who delay their prayer from its fixed times:

﴿ فَوَيْلٌ لِّلْمُصَلِّينَ ۝ ٱلَّذِينَ هُمْ عَن صَلَاتِهِمْ سَاهُونَ ﴾

"So woe unto those performers of prayers (hypocrites), who delay their prayer from its stated fixed time," (V.107:4,5)

Rules of *Salât* (Prayer)

1. Purification.

Before a Muslim starts his prayer, he should purify himself by cleaning his excretion organs if he had urinated

51

or evacuated his bowels. Then he performs *Wudû* (ablution).

The first step in performing ablution is to intend it. There is no need to express the intention in a loud voice, but it is enough to intend it by heart, because Allah knows the intention of His bondsmen. The Prophet ﷺ used not to utter words expressing his intention for ablution. Thus, every Muslim should follow his way.

The worshipper continues his ablution by rinsing his mouth with water thrice, sniffing water up his nostrils and blowing it out thrice, washes his face three times making sure that the water reaches all the parts of his face. After washing the face, the worshipper washes his hands, arms up to the elbows, the right hand before the left, then, wipes his head with his hands starting from front to back and vice versa, rubs his ears and finally washes his feet up to his ankle three times, the right leg before the left leg. A Muslim should keep up his ablution. If he urinates after ablution, evacuates his bowels, passes wind or loses his consciousness for any reason, he should reperform ablution to clean himself again before performing prayer.

If a Muslim is in a state of major impurity, (discharge of semen in erotic dreams or sexual intercourse .... etc), he should clean his body by taking a bath. Women also should carry out this cleansing bath to purify themselves after menstruation or childbirth. Allah has disburdened women and exempted them from performing prayer during menstruation and childbirth periods. As for other times, they are required to perform prayer promptly.

If a Muslim is in a deserted area or on a journey and finds no water, or if he fears that using water will harm him (because of sickness), he is permitted to purify himself by using good clean earth or sand instead of water. This is called *Tayammum* or purification with earth. It is done in the following way: You intend by heart to perform it. Then you strike the dust (or sand) with your hands and wipe your right hand over your face, over the back of your right hand by your left hand and over the back of your left hand by your right hand. Purification with earth is also permissible to women after the period of menstruation or confinement if water is not available, or if its use could harm them.

2.   How to perform *Salât* (Prayer)?

The morning prayer consists of two *Rak'a* (prayer units).A Muslim, whether a man or a woman, stands facing the *Qiblah*, (turning his face and whole body towards the Ka'ba, the Sacred House of Allah in Makka), then he intends by heart without uttering his intention that he will perform the morning prayer and starts it by saying:

Allahu Akbar which means: «اللهُ أَكْبَرُ» "Allah is Great."

The worshipper recites after that this opening prayer:

«سُبْحَانَكَ اللَّهُمَّ وَبِحَمْدِكَ وَتَبَارَكَ اسْمُكَ، وَتَعَالَىٰ جَدُّكَ
وَلَا إِله غَيْرُكَ»

which means: "Praise and Glory be to Allah. Blessed be Your Name. Exalted be Your Majesty and Glory. There is no God save You".

After reciting the opening invocation, the worshipper says:

«أَعُوذُ بِاللهِ مِنَ الشَّيْطَانِ الرَّجِيْمِ»

which means: "I seek the protection of Allah from the accursed Satan". Then, he recites *Fâtiha*, or the opening

Sûrah of the Qur'ân:

بِسْمِ ٱللَّهِ ٱلرَّحْمَٰنِ ٱلرَّحِيمِ ٥ ٱلْحَمْدُ لِلَّهِ رَبِّ ٱلْعَٰلَمِينَ ٥ ٱلرَّحْمَٰنِ ٱلرَّحِيمِ ٥ مَٰلِكِ يَوْمِ ٱلدِّينِ ٥ إِيَّاكَ نَعْبُدُ وَإِيَّاكَ نَسْتَعِينُ ٥ ٱهْدِنَا ٱلصِّرَٰطَ ٱلْمُسْتَقِيمَ ٥ صِرَٰطَ ٱلَّذِينَ أَنْعَمْتَ عَلَيْهِمْ غَيْرِ ٱلْمَغْضُوبِ عَلَيْهِمْ وَلَا ٱلضَّآلِّينَ

The meaning of this Glorious *Sûrah* can be translated as follows:

"In the Name of Allah, the Most Beneficent, the Most Merciful. All the praises and thanks be to Allah, the Lord of the *'Alamîn* (mankind, jinns and all that exists). The Most Beneficent, the Most Merciful. The Only Owner (and the Only Ruling Judge) of the Day of Recompense (i.e. the Day of Resurrection). You (Alone) we worship, and You (Alone) we ask for help (for each and everything). Guide us to the Straight Way. The Way of those on whom You have bestowed Your Grace, not (the way) of those who earned Your Anger (such as the Jews), nor of those who went astray (such as the Christians)." (V.1:1-7)

These verses of Qur'ân, and all other verses, should be recited in Arabic language![1]

---

[1] If in praying one recites the Qur'ân in a language other than Arabic, what he recites will not be of the Qur'ân but it will be a translation of the meaning of the Qur'ân. One of the main characteristics of the Qur'ân is that it is in Arabic, and any translation of its words from Arabic into any other language takes away its glamorous eloquent literature and wondrous nature. Thus, reciting Qur'ân, especially in prayers, can never be in any language other than Arabic.

54

After reciting the *Fâtiha*, the worshipper recites also a passage containing at least three verses of the Qur'ân, or a *Sûrah* like *Sûrat Ikhlâs*. Then he bows saying:

«اللهُ أَكْبَرُ»

which means: "Allah is Great." Bending his head and back and putting his hands on the knees. While bowing one should say thrice:

«سُبْحَانَ رَبِّيَ الْعَظِيْمِ»

which means: "Our Lord, praise is for Thee Alone." Then, he says *Allahu Akbar* and prostrates in a *Sajdah* placing his hands, his knees, forehead, nose and his tiptoes on the ground. He recites thrice while in prostration:

«سُبْحَانَ رَبِّيَ الأَعْلىٰ»

which means: "Glorified is my Exalted Lord."

Then, the worshipper assumes the erect sitting position saying *Allahu Akbar* and says while sitting:

«رَبِّيَ اغْفِرْ لِيْ»

which means: "O my Lord, forgive me."

He prostrates again saying:

«اللهُ أَكْبَرُ»

and repeats what he said during the first prostration:

«سُبْحَانَ رَبِّيَ الأَعْلىٰ»

which means: "Glorified is my Exalted Lord". The worshipper stands upright again saying *Allah Akbar*:

«اللهُ أَكْبَرُ»

recites the *Fâtiha* and some other verses of the Qur'ân,

55

bowing prostrating and repeating what he did and said during the first *Rak'a* (the unit of prayer).

However after the second prostration, instead of standing up, he should sit upright to recite the *Tashahhud* as follows:-

«التَّحِيَّاتُ لله، والصَّلَوَاتُ والطَّيِّبَاتُ السَّلَامُ عَلَيْكَ أَيُّهَا النَّبِيُّ وَرَحْمَةُ اللهِ وَبَرَكَاتُهُ، السَّلَامُ عَلَيْنَا وَعَلَى عِبَادِ اللهِ الصَّالِحِينَ، أَشْهَدُ أَنْ لَا إِلهَ إِلَّا اللهُ، وَأَشْهَدُ أَنَّ مُحَمَّدًا عَبْدُهُ وَرَسُوْلُهُ، اللَّهُمَّ صَلِّ عَلَى مُحَمَّدٍ، وَعَلَى آلِ مُحَمَّدٍ كَمَا صَلَّيْتَ عَلَى إِبْرَاهِيْمَ، وَعَلَى آلِ إِبْرَاهِيْمَ إِنَّكَ حَمِيْدٌ مَجِيْدٌ»

which means: "All service, all worship and all sanctity are for Allah. Peace be upon you, O Prophet, and Allah's Mercy and Blessings. Peace be upon us and upon those who practise righteousness. I bear witness that there is no god but Allah, and I bear witness that Muhammad is His servant and Messenger. O Allah, have mercy on Muhammad and those related to Muhammad, just as You had mercy on Ibrâhîm and on those related to Ibrâhîm; surely You are the Praiseworthy, the Great. O Allah, bestow Your Blessings on Muhammad and on those related to Muhammad as You had bestowed it on Ibrâhîm and those related to Ibrâhîm. Surely, You are the Praiseworthy, the Great."

Then the worshipper turns his face to the right saying:-

«السَّلَامُ عَلَيْكُمْ وَرَحْمَةُ اللهِ»

which means: "Peace be upon you and Allah's Mercy too"

and turns his face to the left saying the same words. This brings the two *Rak'a* of the morning prayer (*Fajr*) to completion.

As for noon (*Zuhr*), afternoon (*'Asr*) and the night (*'Ishâ'*) prayers, each one of these consists of four *Rak'a* (four units of prayer bows.) The first two *Rak'a* of these prayers are performed in the same manner as the morning prayer. But after reciting the *Tashahhud*, the worshipper should not turn his head to the right and left to say, "*As-Salamu Alaikum.*" Instead, he stands up and continues to pray the third and fourth *Rak'a*, then, sitting after the fourth *Rak'a*, he recites the *Tashahhud* again, asks Allah to have Mercy on Muhammad صلى الله عليه وسلم , then he terminates his prayer by turning his face first to the right, then to the left saying in each time, "*As-Salamu 'Alaikum wa Rahmatuallah,*" which means: "Peace be upon you and Allah's Mercy too."

As for the *Maghrib* prayer (evening prayer) it consists of three *Rak'a* (three units of prayer), the first two *Rak'a* are performed in the same manner as that mentioned before for the noon prayer, then the worshipper stands up and performs a third *Rak'a*. After that, he sits upright, recites the *Tashahhud* and terminates his prayer by the *Tasleem*, (*As-Salamu 'Alaikum.*) It is advisable to the worshipper to repeat, in bowing and prostrating, the words by which he Glorifies Allah.

Muslims males should perform the five daily prayers in congregation in a mosque. An *Imâm* leads Muslims in congregational prayers. Muslims select their *Imâm* on the basis that he should be the most pious among them, the best in reciting and understanding the meaning of Qur'ânic verses and the best among them in performing the prayers perfectly. The *Imâm* recites the *Fâtiha* and

57

other Qur'ânic verses in a loud voice in the two *Rak'a* of the morning prayer, the first two *Rak'a* of the evening and *'Ishâ'* prayer.

A female Muslim performs prayer alone or in congregation. She should veil her whole body including the hands and feet in order to protect her pudency and not to allure men. It is permissible for her to unveil her face only when she prays alone and she must cover her face if she is in the presence of a man. When she prays in a mosque, she must be veiled, not perfumed and perform her prayers behind men.

The Muslim performs his prayers in complete humility and submissiveness to Allah. He should go to his prayers peacefully and be tranquil in bowing and prostration. He should avoid haste, amusement and raising his eyes up to the sky and must not utter anything during his prayers other than the Qur'ânic verses and the rites of his prayer.

On Fridays, Muslims perform in congregation the *Jumu'ah* prayer (Friday prayer). It consists of two *Rak'a* in which the *Imâm* recites the *Fâtiha* and Qur'ânic verses aloud. This prayer is preceded by two sermons in which the *Imâm* preaches to the Muslims, instructs them and reminds them to behave according to the precepts of their religion. Friday congregational prayer is obligatory on men, they must attend it on Fridays at noon.

The *Zakât* (Obligatory Charity)

The third pillar of Islâm: paying the poor-due:

Allah ordained every Muslim who possesses a certain amount of property, to pay annually the *Zakât* (poor-due), of his possessions to the poor or to the other categories of people mentioned in the Qur'ân.

The minimum amount of gold liable to payment of *Zakât* is 20 *Mithqâl* of gold (a *Mithqâl* is a weight equal to 4.68 grams) and the minimum amount of silver is 200 *Dirham* (a *Dirham* is a weight that equals 3.12 grams) or an equivalent sum of current money to this amount.

There is also a minimum amount for goods of commerce liable to payment of *Zakât*. As for cereals and grains, its minimum amount is 300 *Sâ'* (a *Sâ'* is a cubic measure used by Arabs.) The minimum amount for real estates prepared for sale should be estimated in accordance with its value, but if the real estate is prepared for lease, the estimation should be in accordance with its rent.

The annual amount of *Zakât* fixed on gold, silver and goods of commerce is 2.5%. As for cereals, grains and fruits, the fixed amount of *Zakât* is 10% of the crop, if the crop is the yield of an easily irrigated land (i.e. a land irrigated by river, spring or rain), but if the land is irrigated with difficulty (i.e. by man-made means such as pumps or other lifting apparatus), the amount of *Zakât* becomes only 5%. *Zakât* of grains, fruits and crops is due at the harvest time. In case of a land that yields two or three harvests annually, one should pay the *Zakât* for each harvest independently.

The amount of *Zakât* due on camels, cows and sheep is explained in books dealing with this subject.

Zakât is enjoined by the Qur'ân:

﴿ وَمَآ أُمِرُوٓاْ إِلَّا لِيَعْبُدُواْ ٱللَّهَ مُخْلِصِينَ لَهُ ٱلدِّينَ حُنَفَآءَ وَيُقِيمُواْ ٱلصَّلَوٰةَ وَيُؤْتُواْ ٱلزَّكَوٰةَ وَذَٰلِكَ دِينُ ٱلْقَيِّمَةِ ﴾

"And they were commanded not, but that they should worship Allah, and worship none but Him

Alone (abstaining from ascribing partners to Him), and offer prayers perfectly (*Iqâmat-as-Salât*) and give *Zakât,* and that is the right religion." (V.98:5)

In fact *Zakât* has a wonderful social role. It soothes the poor's feelings, satisfies their needs, and strengthens the bonds of mutual love among the poor and the rich.

Zakât is not the only means that Islâm has used to maintain social solidarity and co-operation among Muslims, but Islâm also imposes on the rich to support the poor at times of famines. Islâm prohibits the Muslim from being sated with food while his neighbour is hungry. Islâm enjoined also *Zakât-al-Fitr* (*Fitr* — fast-due) on all Muslims and has made it a duty on everyone of them to distribute a *Sâ'* (a cubic measure) of elementary substances for himself and a similar *Sâ'* for each one of those whom he supports, including his servants. The whole amount should be distributed among the poor, before the prayer of feast day. Islâm imposed also expiatory gifts on the Muslim who commits perjury (that is to feed ten poor people or clothe them or to fast three days, if he is unable to feed or clothe the poor). The Muslim is commanded to perform his vows, and practise voluntary charity. Allah promised to give the best rewards for those who expend their money for His sake. Their rewards will not only be multiplied to tenfold, but to 700 folds, or even to a boundless number.

Saum (fasts) of the Month of Ramadan

The fourth pillar of Islâm is to fast during the month of Ramadan, the ninth month of the *Hijri* calendar.

Before the dawn of the first day of Ramadan, a Muslim intends to fast this month, and abstains every day from drinking, eating, or practising sex till sunset. He performs fast till the end of the month of Ramadan, fulfilling by that the commandment of Allah, and seeking His pleasure.

Fasting has innumerable benefits. When a man refrains himself from lust, abstains from eating and drinking for the sake of Allah, he does this only for one purpose; that is to obey Allah, worship Him and imbue his heart with God's fear.

Fasting has also innumerable hygienic, economic and social benefits which are perceived only by those who perform it with strong belief and sincere faith. The Qur'ân states:-

﴿ يَٰٓأَيُّهَا ٱلَّذِينَ ءَامَنُوا۟ كُتِبَ عَلَيْكُمُ ٱلصِّيَامُ كَمَا كُتِبَ عَلَى ٱلَّذِينَ مِن قَبْلِكُمْ لَعَلَّكُمْ تَتَّقُونَ ٠ أَيَّامًا مَّعْدُودَٰتٍ ... الى قوله تعالى ... وَلِتُكْمِلُوا۟ ٱلْعِدَّةَ وَلِتُكَبِّرُوا۟ ٱللَّهَ عَلَىٰ مَا هَدَىٰكُمْ وَلَعَلَّكُمْ تَشْكُرُونَ ﴾

"O you who believe! Fasting is prescribed for you as it was prescribed for those before you, that you may become *Al-Muttaqûn* (the pious). [Observing *Saum* (fasts)] for a fixed number of days, but if any of you is ill or on a journey, the same number (should be made up) from other days. And as for those who can fast with difficulty, (e.g. an old man, etc.), they have (a choice either to fast or) to feed a *Miskîn* (poor person) (for every day). But whoever does good of his own accord, it is better for him. And that you fast, it is better for you if only you know. The month of Ramadan in which was revealed the Qur'ân, a guidance for mankind and clear proofs for the guidance and the criterion (between right and

61

wrong). So whoever of you sights (the crescent on the first night of) the month (of Ramadan i.e. is present at his home), he must fast that month, and whoever is ill or on a journey, the same number (of days which one did not fast must be made up) from other days. Allah intends for you ease, and He does not want to make things difficult for you. (He wants that you) must complete the same number (of days), and that you must magnify Allah [i.e. to say *Takbîr* (*Allahu-Akbar;* Allah is the Most Great) on seeing the crescent of the months of Ramadan and Shawwal] for having guided you so that you may be grateful to Him." (V.2:183-185)

According to the rules of Qur'ân and Prophetic traditions, it is permissible for a sick man, a man travelling on a journey, a menstruating woman, or a confined woman not to fast, but to make up for what they missed.

Foster-mothers and pregnant women are also permitted not to fast if fasting will harm them or their babies, but they should compensate this fully by fasting for equal number of days. If a man drinks or eats absentmindedly while fasting, he should spit out whatever is still in his mouth as soon as he remembers that he is fasting. In this case his fast is not broken. This is a privilege with which the Muslim nation has been endowed: "Allah forgives sins committed by mistake, forgetfulness, or by compulsion."

Hajj (Pilgrimage)

Pilgrimage (*Hajj*) is the fifth pillar of Islâm. It is a duty of a Muslim to perform pilgrimage to the House of Allah once in a lifetime, but it is permissible for him to go on pilgrimage voluntarily more than once.

Pilgrimage has innumerable benefits:

1. In fulfilling this service, man expresses his devotion to Allah, not only by performing rites which need physical effort, but he expresses also his deep spiritual devotion to Allah and spends of his money for His sake.

2. Pilgrimage is an annual Muslim congress, attended by Muslims from all over the world.

They meet in one place, Makka; all being dressed in one uniform, worshipping Allah, the One God and performing the same rites during the fixed period of *Hajj*. There is no discrimination between them; all are Allah's bondsmen; no white man has preference over a black man, neither the rich over the poor. In this way, Muslims are acquainted with one another, co-operate one with the other, and they remember the day when they will be resurrected and gathered before Allah who will account them for their deeds. Thus, they prepare themselves for the Hereafter and do their best to obey Allah, their Lord.

The Ka'ba is the *Qiblah* of all Muslims, they direct their faces towards it when they perform their prayers. But, it should be well-known that all the rites of pilgrimage such as circumambulating round the Ka'ba, attending 'Arafat, Muzdalifa, and staying for several days in Mina .... all these rites have one objective .... that is to worship Allah according to the method He commanded and during the time He fixed. Worshipping is neither dedicated to the Ka'ba nor to any of these other places which are no more than objects created by Allah that can never bring benefit or cause harm to anyone. Worshipping is dedicated to Allah Alone, The Lord of everything, Who Alone has the absolute sovereignty and all power.

According to the Muslim's faith, all forms of worshipping

63

are enjoined by Allah and should never be based on individual judgement or taste. Therefore, had Allah not commanded people to perform pilgrimage to the Sacred House at Makka, Muslims would have never performed it. Evidence for pilgrimage from the Qur'ân :

$$\text{﴿ وَلِلَّهِ عَلَى ٱلنَّاسِ حِجُّ ٱلْبَيْتِ مَنِ ٱسْتَطَاعَ إِلَيْهِ سَبِيلًا وَمَن كَفَرَ فَإِنَّ ٱللَّهَ غَنِيٌّ عَنِ ٱلْعَٰلَمِينَ ﴾}$$

"... And *Hajj* (pilgrimage to Makka) to the House is a duty that mankind owes to Allah, those who can afford the expenses (for one's conveyance, provision and residence); and whoever disbelieves [i.e. denies *Hajj* (pilgrimage to Makka), then he is a disbeliever of Allah], then Allah stands not in need of any of the *'Alâmin* (mankind and jinns)." (V.3:97)

Performing *'Umra* or lesser pilgrimage once in a lifetime is also a duty that a Muslim should fulfil either during *Hajj* time or at any other time.

It is not an indispensable duty for every Muslim to visit the mosque of the Prophet in Al-Madina during *Hajj* time or at any other time, but this is an advisable deed and whoever performs it will be rewarded by Allah. The tradition which states:

$$\text{« مَنْ حَجَّ فَلَمْ يَزُرْنِي فَقَدْ جَفَانِي »}$$

"Whoever performs pilgrimage and does not visit me is turning away from me"

is untrue and is imputed falsely to the Prophet.

A Muslim leaving for Madina intends to visit the mosque of the Prophet. When he arrives there, he prays in the mosque and then visits the tomb of the Prophet صلى الله عليه وسلم. The visitor salutes the Prophet politely and leaves the place in the same manner as the Companions of the

Prophet used to do. He should not ask the Prophet or supplicate for anything from him. In fact those who supplicate the Prophet for help, ask him for what they need, or invoke him to be their intercessor to Allah, are committing idolatry and the Prophet is innocent of their ill-deed. Therefore, every Muslim should be aware to avoid such idolatrous deeds.

After visiting the Prophet's mosque, the visitor also visits the graveyard at Baqi'. He should behave during his visit in conformity with Islâmic ethics and invoke Allah to bless the deads and martyrs buried in these tombs.

The manner of performing *Hajj* And *'Umra*

A Muslim who intends to perform *Hajj* or *'Umra* should expend in this journey of his pure and lawful wealth and avoid using illicit gains lest it should ruin his pilgrimage. The Prophet صلى الله عليه وسلم said:

$$ «كُلُّ لَحْمٍ نَبَتَ مِنْ سُحْتٍ فَالنَّارُ أَوْلَى بِهِ» $$

"Whatever flesh that comes to grow out of illicit gains is rather doomed to Hell-fire".

It is also advisable for a pilgrim to select a man of good faith to accompany him on pilgrimage.

A pilgrim, whether travelling by car or train, puts on *Ihrâm* as soon as he arrives at the *Miqât* (the station for *Ihrâm*), and a pilgrim, travelling by plane, puts on *Ihrâm* when he approaches the *Miqât*. According to Prophetic traditions, there are five *Mawâqît* (five stations for *Ihrâm*):

1. Dhul Hulaifa (Abyar Ali) : for pilgrims from Al-Madina.

2. Al-Juhfa, a place near Rabigh, for people coming from the directions of Syria, Egypt and Maghrib.

3. Qarn Al-Manâzil, for people coming from Najd, At-Tâ'if and other regions of that direction.

4. Dhat Irq, for people coming from Iraq.

5. Yalamlam, for people coming from Yemen. These *Mawâqit* are not only for people coming from the above-mentioned regions, but also for those who chance to travel by these routes.

As for the inhabitants of Makka and those who live within the area bounded by these *Mawâqit*, they assume their *Ihrâm* from their homes.

Manner of *Ihrâm*

It is advisable for a pilgrim to take a bath, to clean and perfume himself before assuming *Ihrâm* at the *Miqât*. The *Ihrâm* dress for males consists of two simple white seamless sheets, one to be wrapped round the loins and the other to cover the upper part of the body. The head should not be covered. Women have no special dress for *Ihrâm*, but they should be dressed in wide veiling and unalluring clothes. After assuming the *Ihrâm*, a woman should neither veil her face with a seamed veil, nor use any seamed gloves to cover her hands. It is permissible for her to cover her face with a part of her head-veil if she finds herself surrounded by men, the same manner adopted before by the wives of the Prophet صلى الله عليه وسلم and the wives of his Companions.

The pilgrim, after assuming *Ihrâm*, intends by heart to perform '*Umra* and says:

$$ «اللّٰهُمَّ لَبَّيْكَ عُمْرَةً» $$

which means: "O Allah, here I am at Your service intending to perform '*Umra*."

66

In this way the pilgrim performs *Hajj-Tamattu'* which is excellent because the Prophet صلى الله عليه وسلم recommended his Companions to perform this form of *Hajj*. He even obliged them to abandon their *Ihrâm* and make their visit to Ka'ba in *'Umra*, giving exception only to those who brought with them their *Hady* (sacrifices), and carried on their *Hajj* by *Qirân*, the same manner which the Prophet himself adopted. The *Qârin* (who performs *Hajj* by *Qirân*) intends when he starts his pilgrimage rites by saying:-

«اللّٰهُمَّ لَبَّيْكَ عُمْرَةً وَحَجًّا»

"Here I am, O Allah, I intend to perform *Umra* and *Hajj*".

Therefore he should not abandon his *Ihrâm* and all *Ihrâm* restrictions till he offers his sacrifice on the feast-day (Day of Immolation, 10th of *Dhul-Hijja*) called *'Eid-al-Adha*.

After assuming the *Ihrâm*:

1. It is forbidden for a Muslim to cohabit with his wife, kiss, or touch her lustfully. During the *Ihrâm* period a pilgrim is also not allowed to marry or propose to a lady.

2. It is also forbidden for a Muslim to remove or trim his hair from any part of the body.

3. Similarly, paring the nails of hands and toes is also forbidden.

4. A man in *Ihrâm* should not cover his head, but it is permissible for him to be shaded by an umbrella or sit in the shade of a tent.

5. During the *Ihrâm* one is not allowed to apply perfume to his body or garments or even to smell it.

6. It is forbidden during the *Ihrâm* to kill animals of game or to help others to do so.

7. A male pilgrim is not allowed to wear tailored clothes during the period of *Ihrâm*; instead of shoes he can use sandals. Women should not wear seamed veils on their faces.

As soon as the pilgrim arrives at the Ka'ba, the Sacred House of Allah, he circumambulates it seven times for the *Tawâf-al-Qudûm*, (circumambulation of arrival). He starts the *Tawâf* from near the Black Stone. That is his *'Umra Tawâf*; the pilgrim can invoke Allah by whatever prayers he likes. After completing the seven rounds of *Tawâf* he moves to the station of Ibrâhim, where or somewhere in the vicinity, he performs a two *Rak'a* prayer of the *Tawâf*.

A pilgrim proceeds after that for *Sa'y*. He starts by mounting the eminence As-Safa and faces the *Qiblah* saying *Allahu Akbar, La ilaha illa-Allah,* and invokes Allah by whatever prayers he likes. Then, he walks to the eminence of Al-Marwa, mounts it, faces the *Qiblah*, saying *Allahu Akbar*, invokes Allah, then returns to the eminence of As-Safa, then repeats this walking from Safa to Marwa and vice versa, till he completes seven rounds at Al-Marwa.

A pilgrim who performs pilgrimage by *Tamattu'*, gets his hair shaven or trimmed after completing his *Sa'y*. For women, it is enough to trim a small part of their hair as long as a finger-tip.

In this way the pilgrim completes his *'Umra,* discards his *Ihrâm* and is free to lead a normal life in all respects

If a woman menstruates or gives birth before or after her *Ihrâm*, she becomes *Qârinah* and performs *Hajj* by *Qirân*. Therefore, she should intend to perform *Hajj* and *'Umra* combined in one *Ihrâm*. Menstruation and confinement do not forbid a woman from doing any of the acts of *Hajj*

68

except the circumambulation of the Sacred House which she should postpone until she becomes clean.

If she gets clean before people assume their *Ihrâm*, she takes a cleansing bath, joins them when they assume their *Ihrâm*, and performs with them the rituals of *Hajj*. But if her cleansing from menses occurs at a later time, following her assuming *Ihrâm*, she combines *Hajj* and *'Umra* in one *Ihrâm*, performs all the rituals of *Hajj*, including staying in Mina, standing in Arafat, going to Muzdalifa, pelting, offering the sacrifice and trimming her hair on feast-day, but she can not circumambulate the Sacred House till she is clean. When she gets clean, she takes a cleansing bath and performs circumambulation round the Ka'ba and *Sa'y*, hence, fulfilling both *Hajj* and *'Umra*. This was the method adopted by the Mother of Believers, 'Aisha رضى الله عنها, according to the directions of the Prophet صلى الله عليه وسلم. The Prophet affirmed by his deeds and sayings that the *Qârin* combines *Hajj* and *'Umra* and fulfils them both by performing one circumambulation and one *Sa'y*. The Prophet himself performed *Hajj* in accordance with this manner and said that *'Umra* is included in *Hajj* till Doomsday.

On the 8th day of *Dhul-Hijja*, the pilgrims assume *Ihrâm* from their settlements in Makka in the same manner they had done before at the *Miqât*. A pilgrim, whether a man or a woman, intends to perform *Hajj* by saying:

«اللّٰهُمَّ لَبَّيْكَ حَجًّا»

"Here I am my Lord, I intend to perform *Hajj*."

A pilgrim refrains himself from practising any of the actions forbidden during the *Ihrâm* period in the same way as explained before. Then he proceeds with other pilgrims to Mina to pass the night there. A pilgrim should perform his prayers there in time. He is permitted to shorten his prayers but not to combine one of them with the other. On the morning of Arafat (the 9th of *Dhul-Hijja*), the pilgrims go to Namira mosque to perform in congregation the *Zuhr* (noon) and *'Asr* (afternoon) prayers combined together. By noon, they proceed to Arafât to stay there till sunset praying, supplicating Allah and asking Him for forgiveness. The pilgrim can stand at any place in the valley of Arafât because the whole of Arafât is reserved for *Wuqûf* (standing). He should turn his face while praying and supplicating towards the *Qiblah* and not towards the mount of Arafât. The pilgrim should be aware that climbing the mount is not a ritual service, and that wiping oneself with its stones is a heretical deed.

After sunset, the pilgrims proceed to Muzdalifa where they perform *Maghrib* (evening) and *'Ishâ* (night) prayers combined together, and shortening only *'Ishâ* prayer. They spend the night there, and next day they perform the *Fajr* (morning) prayer at dawn and leave to Mina before sunrise. When they arrive there, they pelt *Jamrat-al-'Aqaba* by seven pebbles, each one of which should not be larger than a chickpea. One should observe strictly the guidance and orders of the Prophet to overcome the allurement of the Satan and avoid such devious actions as pelting the *Jamra* by shoes and any other action which is not in accordance with the commandments of Allah or the traditions of the Prophet صلى الله عليه وسلم.

After pelting *Jamrat-al-'Aqaba*, the pilgrim offers his sacrifice, then shaves or shortens his hair, (it is better to have it shaven rather than having it shortened). Women slightly trim off parts of their hair.

After that, the pilgrim can discard *Ihrâm* and perform all

the acts which were forbidden during the *Ihrâm* period except sexual intercourse. Then the pilgrim heads for Makka, performs *Tawâf Al-Ifâdah*, and the *Sa'y*, hence, discarding *Ihrâm* completely and he is then allowed to perform all the acts that were forbidden during the *Ihrâm* period with no exception.

The pilgrim returns to Mina, to stay there for three successive days (the feast day and the following two days). He spends the nights of these days at Mina and at every noon or mid-day he pelts the three *Jamarât* (on the 11th and 12th of *Dhul-Hijja*). He starts by pelting *Al-Jamrat-as-Sughra* (the small *Jamra*), then *Al-Jamrat-al-Wusta* (the medium *Jamra*) and finally *Jamrat-al-Aqaba* (the big *Jamra*), which he had pelted before on the morning of the feast day. Each one of these *Jamrât* is pelted by seven pebbles. The pilgrim has the choice after that, either to leave Mina on the 12th of *Dhul-Hijja* or stay there till next day. It is better to stay till next day and perform a pelting at noon. The final thing that a pilgrim should do before leaving Makka, is to perform *Tawâf Al-Wadâ'* (*Tawâf* of departure). However, a woman in a state of menstruation or childbirth is allowed to leave Makka without performing *Tawaf-al-Wadâ'*.

Offering the sacrifice can be done also on 11th, 12th or 13th of *Dhul-Hijja*, and *Tawaf-al-Ifâda* can also be postponed till the pilgrim leaves Mina, but it is better to perform the rituals in accordance with the order and times which are mentioned above.

Faith

The Muslim is ordained to believe not only in Allah, His Messengers and fundamentals of Islâm, but he should also

71

believe in His Angels[1] and the Books which He had revealed to His Messengers.

The Qur'ân is the last Divine Book. It abrogates, substitutes, and stands to preserve the truth of the old Scriptures from corruption. A Muslim should not only believe in Muhammad صلى الله عليه وسلم but he should also believe in all former Prophets whose names have been given in the Qur'ân. The Muslim's faith is that Muhammad صلى الله عليه وسلم is the last of the Messengers of Allah and that he is sent to all nations including Jews, Christians and other sects. Thus, all people should believe in Muhammad صلى الله عليه وسلم and follow him. He who does not believe in him and in Islâm, is disbelieving not only in Muhammad صلى الله عليه وسلم, but also in all other Messengers of Allah, even though he may claim to be a follower of one of them. Moses, Jesus, and other Messengers of Allah exculpate themselves from those who do not believe in Islâm and in Muhammad. Prophet Muhammad صلى الله عليه وسلم said:

«وَالَّذِي نَفْسِي بِيَدِهِ لَا يَسْمَعُ بِي أَحَدٌ مِنْ هَذِهِ الأُمَّةِ يَهُوْدِيٌّ أَوْ نَصْرَانِيٌّ ثُمَّ يَمُوْتُ وَلَمْ يُؤْمِنْ بِالَّذِي أُرْسِلْتُ بِهِ إِلَّا كَانَ مِنْ أَصْحَابِ النَّارِ» [مُسْلِمٌ]

"By Him, Who has my soul in His Hand, anyone of this community that comes to know about me and dies without believing in my message will dwell in Hell-fire, even if he is a Jew or a Christian."

A Muslim believes also in Resurrection, Reckoning,

---

[1] Angels are creatures whom Allah had created from light. They are many in number and no one can count them save Allah. Some of them are in the heavens, some others are entrusted with mankind.

Requital, Paradise, Hell-fire and Divine Decree.

What does it mean to believe in Divine Decree? It means that Allah knows everything that ever existed in the past, that is existing now, and all that will exist in the future, before He created the heavens and earth. This Divine Knowledge is registered in a Preserved Tablet. Therefore, the Muslim believes strongly that nothing can ever exist except by the Will of Allah.

Allah has created people to worship Him and obey Him. He made His commandments and prohibitions very clear and endowed people with the ability and will to carry out what He enjoined them to do, in order that they may obtain His reward, but those who disobey Him will suffer His punishment.

The volition of man is dependent on the Will of Allah. However, there are certain forms of fate in which man's will has absolutely no role, i.e. misfortunes of life, poverty, sickness .... etc. These forms of fate are imposed on people by the Will of Allah Alone, and man will neither be rewarded nor punished for them, because they are beyond his understanding and will, but if man endures and keeps contented with what Allah had fore-ordained for him, Allah will reward him bountifully.

The pious Muslims achieve the highest rank of faith, dwell in the best positions of the Paradise and are the nearest to the consent of Allah, because they worship Allah, glorify Him, and are always submissive to Him as if they are seeing Him. They never disobey Allah secretly or openly. They believe strongly that Allah watches them wherever they may be, and that any of their deeds, sayings or intentions can never be concealed from Allah. If one of them commits a sin, he repents sincerely to Allah, asks

Him forgiveness and never recommits it. The Qur'ân states:-

﴿ إِنَّ ٱللَّهَ مَعَ ٱلَّذِينَ ٱتَّقَوا۟ وَّٱلَّذِينَ هُم مُّحْسِنُونَ ﴾

"For Allah is with those who restrain themselves, and those who do good." (V.16:128)

Islâm, the Perfect Religion

Allah states in the Glorious Qur'ân :

﴿ ٱلْيَوْمَ أَكْمَلْتُ لَكُمْ دِينَكُمْ وَأَتْمَمْتُ عَلَيْكُمْ نِعْمَتِى وَرَضِيتُ لَكُمُ ٱلْإِسْلَٰمَ دِينًا ﴾

"... This day, I have perfected your religion for you, completed My Favour upon you, and have chosen for you Islam as your religion..." (V.5:3)

Allah also states in the Qur'ân:

﴿ إِنَّ هَٰذَا ٱلْقُرْءَانَ يَهْدِى لِلَّتِى هِىَ أَقْوَمُ وَيُبَشِّرُ ٱلْمُؤْمِنِينَ ٱلَّذِينَ يَعْمَلُونَ ٱلصَّٰلِحَٰتِ أَنَّ لَهُمْ أَجْرًا كَبِيرًا ﴾

"Verily, this Qur'ân guides to that which is most just and right and gives glad tidings to the believers (in the Oneness of Allah and His Messenger, Muhammad صلى الله عليه وسلم etc.) who work deeds of righteousness, that they shall have a great reward (Paradise)." (V.17:9)

Allah said also:-

﴿ وَنَزَّلْنَا عَلَيْكَ ٱلْكِتَٰبَ تِبْيَٰنًا لِّكُلِّ شَىْءٍ وَهُدًى وَرَحْمَةً وَبُشْرَىٰ لِلْمُسْلِمِينَ ﴾

"... And We have sent down to you the Book (the Qur'an) as an exposition of everything, a guidance, a mercy, and glad tidings for those who have submitted themselves (to Allah as Muslims)." (V.16:89)

The Prophet صلى الله عليه وسلم said:

«تَرَكْتُكُمْ عَلَى الْمَحَجَّةِ الْبَيْضَاءِ لَيْلُهَا كَنَهَارِهَا لاَ يَزِيغُ عَنْهَا إِلاَّ هَالِكٌ»

"I have guided you to the right path which is as bright as daylight, thus, whoever deviates from this path is doomed to perdition."

He also said:

«تَرَكْتُ فِيكُم مَا إِنْ تَمَسَّكْتُمْ بِهِ لَنْ تَضِلُّوا أَبَدًا كِتَابَ اللهِ وَسُنَّتِي»

"I have left to you the Book of Allah and my *Sunna*, if you hold fast to them, you will never be mislead."

In the first of the above-mentioned Qur'ânic verses, Allah states that He had perfected the religion of Islâm to be suitable and corresponding to the needs of mankind in every place, time and nation. Islâm is not only free from all defects, but, it also corresponds to the needs of mankind and does not impose any unnecessary burden on people. Allah stated also that He had completed His blessings for the Muslim nation by bestowing upon them this perfect, magnanimous and great religion which forms the message of Muhammad صلى الله عليه وسلم, the last Prophet of Allah. Allah promised to give help and victory to Islâm over all enemies, and stated that He had chosen it to be the religion of mankind, and that any other religion, whatever it may be, will not gain His acceptance.

The second verse indicates that the Noble Qur'ân is a clear and perfect method of life which guides people to true solutions for both mundane and religious problems. Whatever a deed may be, the Qur'ân has explained to us whether it may be good or evil. The Qur'ân not only guides us to solutions for all kinds of problems in all times, but the Qur'ânic solutions for these problems are also characterised by being just and right, whereas, all other solutions contrary to it are short-lived and defective as they are based on human feebleness, ignorance and injustice. The Qur'ân is a comprehensive Divine Book which contains the basis of knowledge, faith, politics, system of governing, justice, psychology, sociology, economics, penal law and all sciences that mankind may need. Basics of these fields of knowledge are explained clearly in the Qur'ân and Prophetic traditions. The next chapter will be consecrated to discuss briefly the perfectness of Islâm and its comprehensive method.

Chapter 4
The Method of Islâm

1. Islâm and Science:

According to Islâmic faith, the first commandment of Allah to man is that he must learn and acquire knowledge. Allah stated in the Noble Qur'ân:

﴿ فَٱعْلَمْ أَنَّهُ لَا إِلَٰهَ إِلَّا ٱللَّهُ وَٱسْتَغْفِرْ لِذَنۢبِكَ وَلِلْمُؤْمِنِينَ وَٱلْمُؤْمِنَٰتِ وَٱللَّهُ يَعْلَمُ مُتَقَلَّبَكُمْ وَمَثْوَىٰكُمْ ﴾

"So know (O Muhammad صلى الله عليه وسلم) that *La ilâha illa-Allah*(none has the right to be worshipped but Allah), and ask forgiveness for your sin, and also for (the sin of) believing men and believing women. And Allah knows well your moving about, and your place of rest (in your homes)." (V.47:19)

The Qur'ân also states:

﴿ وَقُل رَّبِّ زِدْنِي عِلْمًا ﴾

"My Lord! Increase me in knowledge." (V.20:114)

Allah also stated:

﴿ فَسْـَٔلُوٓا۟ أَهْلَ ٱلذِّكْرِ إِن كُنتُمْ لَا تَعْلَمُونَ ﴾

"...so ask the people of the Reminder (Scriptures–the Torah, the Gospel) if you do not know." (V.21:7)

Prophet Muhammad صلى الله عليه وسلم said:

«طَلَبُ الْعِلْمِ فَرِيضَةٌ عَلَى كُلِّ مُسْلِمٍ»

"The search for knowledge is a duty laid on every Muslim."

He also said:

«فَضْلُ الْعَالِمِ عَلَى الْجَاهِلِ كَفَضْلِ الْقَمَرِ لَيْلَةَ الْبَدْرِ عَلَى سَائِرِ الْكَوَاكِبِ»

"The superiority of a scholar over an ignorant man is as obvious as the brightness of the full-moon in dark nights."

Islâm classifies knowledge into two categories:-

a) Obligatory Knowledge:

This is a duty on every Muslim, whether male or female. The Muslim must know Allah, His Messenger Prophet Muhammad صلى الله عليه وسلم and acquire knowledge concerning the fundamentals of Islâm using available evidence.

b) Optional Knowledge:

This is a collective duty, meaning that it is not a duty on every individual, but if a group of individuals in the community undertakes to acquire this kind of knowledge, all other individuals will be exempted from this duty, and the whole community will be free from the responsibility of negligence to acquire this kind of knowledge. Examples of such knowledge are:- to study Islâmic Law, to study other basic sciences, industries, and professions which are of vital necessity for the welfare of the community. Muslim rulers should always do their best to procure scholars, professionals and qualifed men in all fields of optional knowledge to satisfy the needs of the Muslim community.

2. Islâm and Faith:

Allah commanded His Messenger Muhammad صلى الله عليه وسلم

78

to proclaim to all people that they are the bondsmen of Allah Alone, and that they should worship none but Allah. He ordered them to relate themselves with Allah directly without any intercessor between Him and them, that they should put their trust in Him Alone, fear none except Him, and ask for everything from none except Him.

Man must glorify Allah, his Lord by His Holy Attributes and Holy Names. This was the manner of Muhammad صلى الله عليه وسلم. All these meanings have already been exposed and explained in the chapter dealing with the explanation of the meaning of (No god save Allah.)

3. Islâm and Fostering Bonds of Friendship among People:

Allah commanded Muslims to be good and to strive for the deliverance of humanity from the darkness of blasphemy to the light of Islâm. Belief in Allah is the cornerstone on which the Muslim bases his relations with others. He loves the righteous people who obey Allah and His Messenger even if they are not connected with Him by any bond of relation. Allah abominates the disbelievers and those who disobey Him and His Messenger even though they may be his closest relatives. This connection, being based on belief in Allah, not only gathers dispersed groups and unites different communities, but it also survives more than all other human-made bonds such as nationalism, material interests and even blood relationships which are feeble and liable to break down. Allah states in the Qur'ân :

﴿ لَّا تَجِدُ قَوْمًا يُؤْمِنُونَ بِٱللَّهِ وَٱلْيَوْمِ ٱلْأَخِرِ يُوَآدُّونَ مَنْ حَآدَّ ٱللَّهَ وَرَسُولَهُ وَلَوْ كَانُوٓا۟ ءَابَآءَهُمْ أَوْ أَبْنَآءَهُمْ أَوْ إِخْوَٰنَهُمْ أَوْ عَشِيرَتَهُمْ ﴾

"You (O Muhammad صلى الله عليه وسلم) will not find any people who believe in Allah and the Last Day, making friendship with those who oppose Allah and His Messenger (Muhammad صلى الله عليه وسلم), even though they were their fathers, or their sons, or their brothers, or their kindred (people)..." (V.58:22)

Allah also states:

$$﴿ إِنَّ أَكْرَمَكُمْ عِندَ ٱللَّهِ أَتْقَىٰكُمْ ﴾$$

"...Verily, the most honourable of you near Allah is that (believer) who has *At-Taqwa* [i.e. one of the *Muttaqûn*: i.e. pious and righteous persons who fear Allah much (abstain from all kinds of sins and evil deeds which He has forbidden), and love Allah much (perform all kinds of good deeds which He has ordained)]." (V.49:13)

Allah commanded Muslims to do justice to both enemies and friends and forbade all his bondsmen to do injustice to others.

Allah commanded His bondsmen to be honest, truthful, kind to parents, the poor and the benevolent and to desist from all kinds of deception. Allah commanded them to be good in their behaviour towards everything, even towards animals and birds, which they are ordered not to torture in any way. The Muslim is ordered to kill harmful animals and insects like scorpions, serpents, rats, mordacious dogs ... etc, to protect himself and his community, but he is not allowed to torture them.

4. Self-conscientiousness and heart heedfulness of the believer :

The verses of the Glorious Qur'ân inform people that Allah sees His bondsmen wherever they may be, knows all their deeds and intentions and that His angels are accompanying them to register whatever they do openly or secretly. People will have to account for all that they do or say. Allah warns them that they will be punished severely if they disobey His Commandments. This Divine warning refrains the believers and prevents them from disobeying Allah or committing sins and crimes.

As for those who are heedless of Allah's punishment, and are not ashamed of commiting sins whenever they can, Islâm imposes on them certain deterring restrictions:

1. The whole Muslim community is accountable to Allah for preaching good deeds and forbidding indecency. In this way, the Muslim, who does not interfere positively to prevent a man from committing a crime or a sin will be responsible for his negative attitude to Allah.

2. Muslim rulers are commanded to execute the punishments laid down in the Qur'ân against the criminals who commit grievous crimes mentioned therein. The Prophet صلى الله عليه وسلم explained these crimes and carried out such punishments against the sinners during his lifetime.

5. Islâm and Social interdependence :

Allah enjoined Muslims to co-operate with one another in material and moral fields. Some forms of this co-operation have already been explained in the chapter concerning *Zakât*.

A Muslim is not only forbidden to cause harm to others, but he is also commanded to be positive and remove what acts others do that may cause harm to anyone. Removing an obstructing stone from the road, or a thorn from the shade of a tree, although it may appear a trifle deed, yet it is a good action for which a man will be rewarded.

81

It is the duty of a Muslim to wish for his fellow-brother what he wishes for himself, and to dislike for him what he dislikes for himself. The Qur'ân states :-

﴿ وَتَعَاوَنُوا عَلَى ٱلْبِرِّ وَٱلتَّقْوَىٰ وَلَا تَعَاوَنُوا عَلَى ٱلْإِثْمِ وَٱلْعُدْوَانِ ﴾

"... Help you one another in *Al-Birr* and *At-Taqwa* (virtue, righteousness and piety); but do not help one another in sin and transgression." (V.5:2)

The Qur'ân also states:-

﴿ إِنَّمَا ٱلْمُؤْمِنُونَ إِخْوَةٌ فَأَصْلِحُوا بَيْنَ أَخَوَيْكُمْ ﴾

"The believers are nothing else than brothers (in Islamic religion). So make reconciliation between your brothers..." (V.49:10)

﴿ لَا خَيْرَ فِي كَثِيرٍ مِّن نَّجْوَىٰهُمْ إِلَّا مَنْ أَمَرَ بِصَدَقَةٍ أَوْ مَعْرُوفٍ أَوْ إِصْلَاحٍ بَيْنَ ٱلنَّاسِ وَمَن يَفْعَلْ ذَٰلِكَ ٱبْتِغَاءَ مَرْضَاتِ ٱللَّهِ فَسَوْفَ نُؤْتِيهِ أَجْرًا عَظِيمًا ﴾

"There is no good in most of their secret talks save (in) him who orders *Sadaqa* (charity in Allah's Cause), or *Ma'rûf* (Islamic Monotheism and all the good and righteous deeds which Allah has ordained), or conciliation between mankind, and he who does this, seeking the good Pleasure of Allah, We shall give him a great reward." (V.4:114)

Prophet Muhammad صلى الله عليه وسلم said:

«لَا يُؤْمِنُ أَحَدُكُمْ حَتَّى يُحِبَّ لِأَخِيهِ مَا يُحِبُّ لِنَفْسِهِ»

"None of you will be a believer till he wishes for his fellow-brother what he wishes for himself."

In his magnificent farewell speech, which he made at

Arafât before his death, Prophet Muhammad صلى الله عليه وسلم
said:

«يَا أَيُّهَا النَّاسُ إِنَّ رَبَّكُمْ وَاحِدٌ، وَأَبَاكُمْ وَاحِدٌ، أَلاَ لاَ فَضْلَ
لِعَرَبِيٍّ عَلَى عَجَمِيٍّ، وَ لاَ لِعَجَمِيٍّ عَلَى عَرَبِيٍّ، وَلاَ لِأَسْوَدَ
عَلَى أَحْمَرَ، وَلاَ لِأَحْمَرَ عَلَى أَسْوَدَ، إِلاَّ بِالتَّقْوَى، أَبْلَغْتُ؟
قَالُوا أَبْلَغَ رَسُوْلُ اللهِ»

"O people, your Lord is One, and your father is one,
an Arab has no preference over a non-Arab, nor is a
black man privileged over a white man, or a red man
over a black man except in piousness and god-
fearing. Have I informed you?" The people
answered, "Yes you did."

«إِنَّ دِمَاءَكُمْ وَأَمْوَالَكُمْ وَأَعْرَاضَكُمْ عَلَيْكُمْ حَرَامٌ كَحُرْمَةِ
يَوْمِكُمْ هٰذَا فِي شَهْرِكُمْ هٰذَا وَفِي بَلَدِكُمْ هٰذَا أَلاَ هَلْ
بَلَّغْتُ؟ قَالُوا: نَعَمْ. فَرَفَعَ إِصْبَعَهُ إِلَى السَّمَاءِ، وَقَالَ:
اللّٰهُمَّ اشْهَدْ».

"Your lives, your properties and your honour are
as sacred as this day (day of *Hajj*) of this holy month
in this inviolable city (Makka)."

6. Islâm and Domestic Affairs:

Allah commanded the Muslims to appoint from among
themselves an *Imâm* to be their ruler. Muslims should
acknowledge the right of authority of their ruler. They
should also unite in one nation and never disperse. They
are not allowed to disobey their rulers or leaders except in
one case, when the ruler orders them to commit a sin or an
action contrary to the Commandments of Allah.

Allah has commanded the Muslim to emigrate to an Islâmic country if he cannot act on Islâm in his own country, or declare openly there that he is a Muslim. Islâmic countries are the countries ruled by a Muslim ruler and in which all affairs of the community are regulated by the Islâmic Law.

Islâm does not acknowledge territorial boundaries, national or popular relations, and nationalities, as these lead to separation and differentiation among people. There is no nationality for the Muslim except Islâm. According to Islâm, all mankind are Allah's bondsmen, and the whole earth belongs to Allah (not to any nation or a certain country), thus, the Muslim is authorized to migrate wherever he likes as long as he has committed himself to the Laws of Allah. However, if he abrogates these Laws, the penalties stated therein should be inflicted on him. By executing the Laws of Allah, and carrying into force the penalties which He commanded against those who commit certain crimes, the human community can establish security, rightness, and protection of lives, properties and honour. The worst evils befall a community when it abandons these Divine Laws.

Allah prohibited spirits, alcoholic drinks, and drugs of addiction, to preserve for man the faculty of sense with which He endowed him. Whoever drinks wine, any spirits or alcoholic drinks, or takes intoxicating drug is punished according to the Laws of Allah by being flogged from 40 to 80 lashes. This preventive punishment guarantees a wide range of protection for people against all evils and crimes that arise out of alcoholic beverages.

Allah has prescribed retaliation to protect Muslim's lives. He commanded that reprisal and paying back injury for injury should be executed on the intentional murderers and aggressors who kill or wound others intentionally. The Muslim is authorized to practise legitimate self-defence against any aggression on his life, honour, or possessions. Allah stated in the Qur'ân:

﴿ وَلَكُمْ فِى ٱلْقِصَاصِ حَيَوٰةٌ يَتَأُوْلِى ٱلْأَلْبَبِ لَعَلَّكُمْ تَتَّقُونَ ﴾

"And there is (a saving of) life for you in (Al-Qisâs) the Law of Equality in punishment), O men of understanding, that you may become Al-Muttaqûn (the pious)." (V.2:179)

Prophet Muhammad صلى الله عليه وسلم said:

«مَنْ قُتِلَ دُوْنَ نَفْسِهِ فَهُوَ شَهِيْدٌ، وَمَنْ قُتِلَ دُوْنَ أَهْلِهِ فَهُوَ شَهِيْدٌ، وَمَنْ قُتِلَ دُوْنَ مَالِهِ فَهُوَ شَهِيْدٌ».

"Whoever is killed while defending against an attack on his life, his honour, or his possessions, is a martyr."

Allah protected the Muslim's honour by prohibiting calumny and prescribing a punishment against slander and false accusations of fornication or pederasty.

Allah protected man's honour and prevented lineage confusion by preventing adultery and fornication, considering them to be one of the most grievous crimes and prescribing a severe punishment for adulterers and adulteresses.

Allah protected possessions by prohibiting stealing, deception, gambling, bribery and all means of illicit gains. He prescribed severe punishment for thieves and highway robbers, commanding that their hands should be maimed.

All these punishments are enacted by Allah, the All-Wise, the All-Knower. He knows better what suits His bondsmen and puts their society in order. He is the Most-Merciful. These punishments not only expiate the sins of criminals but also protect the whole society against all kinds of evil. Islâm's enemies criticize Islâm for inflicting severe punishments against murderers, robbers and adulterers, but their criticism is null and void because, by inflicting these punishments, Islâm cuts off from the society a vicious spoilt member who, if not punished severely, will spread corruption and viciousness to other members and damage the whole community. Those who criticize Islâm forget that they do not refrain themselves from killing innocents, and encourage all kinds of brutalities in order to achieve their malicious goals.

7. Islâm and Foreign Policy:

Muslims and Muslim rulers are ordained to call people to Islâm to deliver them from the darkness of atheism to the light of faith in Allah, and to rescue them from being immersed in the illusions of the materialistic life wherein they suffer deprivation of spiritual happiness.

One of the grave defects of man-made doctrines is that they preach man to be a good citizen and a useful member only of his own society, whereas, Islâm ordains man to be good and useful to all mankind. This difference proves that Islâm is perfect, magnanimous and superior to all man-made doctrines.

Islâm has its own regulations of war. It demands from Muslims to prepare whatever force they can to protect themselves and their faith, and to dismay the enemies of Allah and their enemies.

However, Allah authorized Muslims to conclude treaties

with non-Muslim nations, on condition that these treaties should be in conformity with Islâmic Law.

Muslims are strictly prohibited to break the treaties which they conclude with their enemies, but they are authorized to abrogate them if the enemy violates these treaties or commits an act contrary to the conditions laid therein.

Muslims are ordained to call their enemies to Islâm before fighting against them. If they refuse, Muslims should call them again to pay the tribute and submit to the Laws of Allah. If the enemy refuses again, Muslims should fight them so that there may be no persecution and religion should be for Allah Alone.

Muslims are strictly commanded not to kill women, children, old men, and monks who do not participate in war against Muslims. They are commanded to treat prisoners of war kindly.

All these commandments prove that the desire for exploitation and domination is not the goal of holy war (*Jihâd*) in Islâm, but its sole aim is to deliver people from man-made-object service to the service of Allah, the Creator. Holy war (*Jihâd*) is only a means to propagate truth and mercy among people.

8.   Islâm and Freedom:

A. Freedom of Faith

In a country ruled by Muslim authorities, a non-Muslim is guaranteed his freedom of faith. He has the full choice, either to embrace Islâm to deliver himself from disbelief and attain prosperity, or to stick to his religion, and hence choose disbelief, distress, and torment in Hell-fire. Such a choice provides a clear-cut evidence against the disbeliever on the day of Judgement. Muslims are forbidden from forcing a non-Muslim to embrace Islâm, but he should pay the tribute to Muslims readily and submissively, surrender to Islâmic Laws, and should not practise his polytheistic rituals openly.

Apostasy from Islâm is a grievous crime punishable by death. One who commits apostasy from Islâm rejects truth after he had known it, thus, he does not deserve life and loses the *raison d'être* of his existence. But if his apostasy is due to a violation of one of the principles of Islâm, he should repent and ask Allah for forgiveness, and behave in accordance with Islâmic rules.

Violations leading to apostasy are of many forms:

1. Idolatry: That is to worship others beside Allah, even if he considers those whom he associates with Allah to be intercessors and not gods (as a symbol of a pious man, or any other creature whom he thinks to be his intercessor to Allah.). Islâm considers one committing such acts to be an idolater or an apostate.

The likeness of those who commit idolatry under the name of intercession is as the likeness of a man who drinks wine after calling it by another name. Allah states in the Qur'ân:

﴿ فَٱعْبُدِ ٱللَّهَ مُخْلِصًا لَّهُ ٱلدِّينَ ○ أَلَا لِلَّهِ ٱلدِّينُ ٱلْخَالِصُ وَٱلَّذِينَ ٱتَّخَذُواْ مِن دُونِهِۦٓ أَوْلِيَآءَ مَا نَعْبُدُهُمْ إِلَّا لِيُقَرِّبُونَآ إِلَى ٱللَّهِ زُلْفَىٰٓ إِنَّ ٱللَّهَ يَحْكُمُ بَيْنَهُمْ فِى مَا هُمْ فِيهِ يَخْتَلِفُونَ إِنَّ ٱللَّهَ لَا يَهْدِى مَنْ هُوَ كَٰذِبٌ كَفَّارٌ ﴾

"So worship Allah (Alone) by doing religious deeds sincerely for Allah's sake only (and not to show off, and not to set up rivals with Him in worship). Surely, the religion (i.e. the worship and the obedience) is for Allah only. And those who take *'Auliyâ'* (protectors and helpers) besides Him (say): 'We worship them only that they may bring us near to Allah.' Verily, Allah will judge between them concerning that wherein they differ. Truly, Allah guides not him who is a liar, and a disbeliever." (V.39:2,3)

Allah also states:-

﴿ ذَٰلِكُمُ ٱللَّهُ رَبُّكُمْ لَهُ ٱلْمُلْكُ وَٱلَّذِينَ تَدْعُونَ مِن دُونِهِۦ مَا يَمْلِكُونَ مِن قِطْمِيرٍ إِن تَدْعُوهُمْ لَا يَسْمَعُواْ دُعَآءَكُمْ وَلَوْ سَمِعُواْ مَا ٱسْتَجَابُواْ لَكُمْ وَيَوْمَ ٱلْقِيَٰمَةِ يَكْفُرُونَ بِشِرْكِكُمْ وَلَا يُنَبِّئُكَ مِثْلُ خَبِيرٍ ﴾

"Such is Allah your Lord; His is the kingdom. And those, whom you invoke or call upon instead of Him, own not even a *Qitmîr* (the thin membrane over the date-stone). If you invoke (or call upon) them, they hear not your call, and if (in case) they were to hear, they could not grant it (your request) to you. And on the Day of Resurrection, they will disown your worshipping them. And none can inform you (O Muhammad صلى الله عليه وسلم) like Him Who is the All-Knower (of each and everything)." (V.35:13,14)

2. The Muslim must charge idolaters, Jews, Christians, atheists and magians with disbelief. He should charge also with disbelief those who worship false deities and take for law, regulations different from those which Allah had revealed. A Muslim commits the grievous sin of disbelief if he does not accuse such men with disbelief.

3. Sorcery is a form of disbelief, especially when it includes grave idolatrous deviation. Therefore, whoever practises sorcery, or gives his consent to such action after knowing that it is atheism is a disbeliever.

4. Whoever believes that there is a law better than the Law of Islâm, or that there is a system better than that revealed to Muhammad صلى الله عليه وسلم , is a disbeliever.

5. Whoever dislikes Prophet Muhammad صلى الله عليه وسلم or abominates any of the rules of Islâmic Law is a disbeliever.

6. Whoever ridicules any of the precepts of Islâm knowingly is a disbeliever.

7. Whoever longs for the defeat of Islâm and abhors its victories is a disbeliever.

8. Whoever takes disbelievers as friends and gives them support knowingly with abrogation to Islâmic Rules is a disbeliever.

9. To believe that there are certain men authorized to violate Islâmic Laws and perform what is contrary to them is disbelief.

10. Whoever shuns Islâmic Faith or law after being reminded of it is a disbeliever.

11. To deny or reject any of the fundamentals of Islâm is disbelief.

All these examples of deviation which lead to apostasy are supported by evidences from the Qur'ân and Prophetic traditions. We should beware of committing any of these deeds.

B. Islâm confers freedom of opinion on Muslims on condition that it should not be used to violate Islâmic precepts. Allah commanded the Muslim to stick to truth and say it wherever he may be heeding no censure of others. This is considered to be one of the highest ranks of fighting in the Cause of Allah. The Muslim should also give good advice to Muslim rulers and admonish them to refrain themselves from all kinds of transgression. Allah ordered Muslims to refute false opinions and restrain those who call people to it from committing this grievous sin.

Such a system based on respecting the opinions of others so long as their opinions are not violating the Law of Allah, is most magnanimous system. Opinions contrary to the Laws of Allah result in nothing but corruption and falsehood, therefore these should not be communicated.

C. Individual liberty is guaranteed in Islâm within the broad limits of Islâmic Laws. Both man and woman have the right to practise all kinds of transaction: i.e. contracts of sale, donation, *Waqf* (trust) etc. As for marriage, both male and female have full liberty to select their spouse, but in exceptional cases, when a female agrees to marry a man who is not equal to her in religious rank (i.e. a man of bad reputation, or negligent of his religious duties such as prayer, fasting etc), the female's father or the most close relative to her has the right to interfere and oppose the marriage with a view to protect her faith, honour and her family's interests. A female should not run about herself to complete marriage formalities, but her legal sponsor should do so on her behalf.

A contract of marriage is dependent on the consent of both the parties (the male and the female). Two witnesses, at least, should be present at the time of concluding the contract and should sign it as witnesses.

According to Islâm, man and whatever he owns belong to

Allah. Therefore, all human behaviour should be within the limits explained by the Commandments of Allah. Islâm permits no transgression or extravagance; the Laws of Allah are not only a guidance to His bondsmen, but they are also a source of mercy on them. To protect the Muslim society from all kinds of abuses and deviations, Islâm has strictly forbidden adultery, fornication, sodomy, suicide and all forms of lewdness.

Allah ordained Muslims to shave off their moustaches, trim their nails, pluck out their armpits and pubic hair and to circumcise males.

Muslims are enjoined not to imitate the behaviour of Allah's enemies, or commit their indecencies. Behaviour-imitation will affect the Muslim's attitudes, and may create in him a sensation of sympathy towards his enemy's indecent mode of life. Allah wants the Muslim to be purged from all vices, and thus be a proper source for original Islâmic thought, independent of all forms of man-made opinions, ideas, or modes of behaviour. The Muslim should be a model for others in both faith and behaviour, he should not be an imitator and dependent on others.

In the field of industries and technical knowledge useful to mankind, Islâm commands the Muslim to strive and acquire this knowledge and experience even from non-Muslims. Knowledge belongs to Allah, and He is the Instructor who provides man with all forms of knowledge. The Noble Qur'ân states:-

$$ ﴿ عَلَّمَ ٱلْإِنسَـٰنَ مَا لَمْ يَعْلَمْ ﴾ $$

"Has taught man that which he knew not." (V.96:5)

This promptness to acquire useful knowledge and science

is the highest rank of reform and admonition for mankind in order to enable man to make use of his liberty, preserve his honour and dignity, and protect himself against evil.

D. Islâm protects man's privacy. It not only prohibits the Muslim from entering into other people's houses without permission, it also interdicts strictly glancing furtively at others inside their dwellings as well as prohibiting all deeds which encroach upon someone's security and right of privacy.

E. Allah has conferred on man the freedom of work. Man has the right to earn and expend within the limits explained by the Laws of Allah. Work is a duty on man. He should work to support himself and his family. But, at the same time, Allah forbids strictly illicit gains which are the outcome of illegal deeds such as usury, gambling, corruption, theft, sorcery etc. Money gained by selling wine, pork, or practising forbidden kinds of entertainment such as singing and dancing is also illicit and prohibited. The Muslim should avoid earning money from illicit sources and should also avoid spending it for ill deeds.

By this method which regulates means of earning and ways of spending, Islâm offers to man the most useful guidance to a prosperous and a happy life.

9. Islâm and Family Status:

Allah organized family status by the Islâmic Law. This perfect Divine organisation ensures happiness for those who adopt it. The Qur'ân and Prophetic traditions call upon and encourage people to marry for many noble reasons.

Marriage is the best means to chastity and protection against indecency. It creates feelings of love and mercy between the couples and ensures security and tranquility for them. Marriage secures also for the society the way to proper growth through chastity and honest legitimate means.

According to Islâm, each couple helps his mate by fulfilling the duties which suit his own nature. The man performs outdoor work to earn money and support his wife and children. The wife undertakes indoor work such as bringing up children well, household management, and doing her best for the happiness of her husband and children.

It is permissible for the wife to work outside her home if her husband allows her to co-operate with him to increase their earnings and support their family. But, there is an important reservation on womens' work outside her home. A female should abstain from performing any work in company with men. Women can perform profitable and productive work in homes, their own farms, or their husbands' or parents' farms. Neither the husband nor the wife's relatives have the right to oblige her to work in company with men in factories, offices, or commercial stores because such co-work will expose her to corruption. A woman secured in her house is protected against all kinds of temptation, but if she leaves her safe shelter to associate with men in works, markets, and other fields of life, she may harm herself and expose her honour and dignity to danger.

Islâm and Polygamy
Polygamy is permissible in Islâm.

Allah authorized man to marry up to four wives, provided that he should treat them all as equals and should not discriminate among them. Islâm considers man responsible for observing equality among his wives in all

94

kinds of material treatment such as equality among them in habitation, clothing and all means of adequate support. But strict equality in emotions and feeling is beyond the control of a man.

Allah states in the Qur'ân:

$$\{ \text{ وَلَن تَسْتَطِيعُوٓاْ أَن تَعْدِلُواْ بَيْنَ ٱلنِّسَآءِ وَلَوْ حَرَصْتُمْ } \}$$

"You will never be able to do perfect justice between wives even if it is your ardent desire."(V.4:129)

The commentators of the Qur'ân are in agreement that this verse refers to equality between wives in emotions and feelings of love. Such equality which is beyond man's ability should not be a reason to justify abolition of polygamy.

Allah authorized His Messengers in all ages to marry more than a wife, because He knows better what is more favourable for His bondsmen. It is a fact that a healthy man can satisfy the sexual desires of four women. Should he restrict himself to only one wife; as Christians and others do, as pretenders of Islâm assert, this will result in many different kinds of corruption:-

1. If the husband is a good believer and obedient to his Lord's Commandments, restricting himself to only one wife will not satisfy his desires, especially in the periods of his wife's menses, childbirth, sickness and during the last months of pregnancy. Certainly he will feel deprivation during these periods.

2. If the husband is a disobedient sinner and does not act according to the commandment of Allah, monogamy may incite him to commit adultery and abondon his wife. The majority of those who oppose polygamy are sinful adulterers who commit fornication and indecency

95

shamelessly with unlimited number of women. A man committing lewdness and fornication while declaring himself to be an open antagonist to polygamy is condemned to be a disbeliever.

3. Monogamy deprives a great number of women of their legitimate right of marriage and having children. In times of wars and disasters, the death rate among men is proportionally high. In these cases, polygamy is the best means to extend the circle of marriage to combine a great number of widows and unmarried women and give them shelter and an honourable life. It is a clear fact that Islâm, by regulating polygamy, has treated women with justice and mercy. Islâm preferred the interests of women as a whole to the individual feeling of jealousy or grief which a wife suffers in case of polygamy. Those who oppose polygamy are the real enemies of women, virtue, and Prophets of Allah. Individual feelings of jealousy should never be taken as a basis to impede laws and systems regulated by Divine Laws.

However, Islâm authorises the wife to stipulate a condition in her marriage contract that she will have the right to be divorced by her own will, if her husband marries a second wife. According to Islâmic Law, the husband has no right in this case to reclaim from his divorced wife the possessions, cash or gifts that he had given her.

Divorce is permissible in Islâm to enable couples to terminate their disputes and unhappy life, so that each one of them may start a new, happier life with a new mate. Divorce in Islâm puts an end to unhappy matrimonial life and removes all deadlock that can prevent people from a happy, honourable life.

10. Islâm and Hygienic Problems:

Many verses of the Qur'ân and Prophetic traditions contain spiritual and material methods for treating many psychological and physical diseases. Allah states in the Qur'ân:

﴿ وَنُنَزِّلُ مِنَ ٱلْقُرْءَانِ مَا هُوَ شِفَآءٌ وَرَحْمَةٌ لِّلْمُؤْمِنِينَ ﴾

"And We send down from the Qur'ân that which is a healing and a mercy to those who believe (in Islamic Monotheism and act on it)..." (V.17:82)

The Prophet صلى الله عليه وسلم said:

«مَا أَنْزَلَ اللهُ مِنْ دَاءٍ إِلاَّ أَنْزَلَ لَهُ دَوَاءً، عَلِمَهُ مَنْ عَلِمَ وَجَهِلَهُ مَنْ جَهِلَ».

"Whatever the disease, Allah has created a medication for it, regardless of the fact that some men may come to know what this medication is and others may not."

The Prophet permitted Muslims to use all kinds of medicines except which contain unlawful elements such as wine, swine-flesh or any other forbidden matter. Ibn Al-Qaiyim treated this subject throughly in his book *Zâd-al-Ma'âd,* so the reader can refer to this book if he wishes to acquire more knowledge on this subject.

11. In addition to hygienic problems, Islâm organises also commerce, economy, industry and agriculture in detail. The Islâmic methods in these fields satisfy properly the needs of people in nutrition and housing, organise public utilities, secure public health in urban and rural societies and maintain the public amenities apparatuses on a proper basis to guarantee the settlement of all social troubles.

12. Muslim's invisible Enemies and the Way to overcome them:

Allah explained to Muslims that they have hidden enemies, who do their best to mislead Muslims to perdition in this worldly life and in the Hereafter. Allah also guided Muslims to the method of delivery from the evils of these unseen enemies. The first of these enemies is the accursed Satan, who stirs up and leads all other enemies of man. Satan was not only a foe to our forefather Adam and our great grandmother Eve, but he is an open enemy of Adam's progeny till the end of this wordly life. Satan strives hard to persuade people either to disbelief or to commit sins in order that they may accompany him in dwelling forever in Hell-fire. Satan is an incorporeal spirit, able to instill evil in man and allure mischief to him as if it were a second nature to him.

Allah explained to us how to overcome Satan and his followers. When a Muslim is about to commit a sin, or when he is maddened with anger, he should say:

«أَعُوذُ بِاللهِ مِنَ الشَّيْطَانِ الرَّجِيْمِ»

"I ask Allah for His refuge against the accursed Satan."

Then he should refrain himself from committing the sin and calm his anger. The Muslim should know that malicious incentives are always motivated by the Satan. Allah said:-

﴿ إِنَّ ٱلشَّيْطَانَ لَكُمْ عَدُوٌّ فَٱتَّخِذُوهُ عَدُوًّا إِنَّمَا يَدْعُواْ حِزْبَهُۥ لِيَكُونُواْ مِنْ أَصْحَابِ ٱلسَّعِيرِ ﴾

"Surely, Satan is an enemy to you, so treat him as an enemy. He only invites his *Hizb* (followers) that they may become the dwellers of the blazing Fire." (V.35:6)

The second foe of man is his lusts. Man can be persuaded to deny the truth and disobey the Commandments of Allah if these are contrary to his lusts. A sinful man always gives priority to emotions and passions over truth and justice. The way to overcome lust is to ask Allah for refuge against one's own lusts, stick to truth, and to refrain from following desires contrary to Allah's Commandments.

The third enemy of man is his base self which incites him to evil. This baserself incites sins and forbidden desires in a man such as drinking wine, committing adultery and breaking fast in Ramadan without a legal excuse. The way to overcome this enemy is to ask Allah for refuge against the baserself and against the devil. Then, one should abstain from committing a sin and strive to gain the refuge of Allah. One should always remind oneself that sinful lusts are evanescent and leave nothing but sorrow and remorse.

Satanic people are the fourth enemy of man. They are called satanic people because they behave like devils, oppose the Commandments of Allah, commit lewdness and tempt people to evil. The best way to overcome this enemy is to remain beware of them and not to associate with them.

13. Islâm, the Noble Aim of this Life and the Way to Happiness :

This worldly life with its evanescent allurements is not the object of a Muslim. Allah explained to Muslims that they should direct their efforts in this life to gain eternity and bliss in the true coming-life, the life after death. This worldly life is not an end in itself; a true Muslim considers it only a means to the life of the Hereafter. Allah stated:

﴿ وَمَا خَلَقْتُ الْجِنَّ وَالْإِنسَ إِلَّا لِيَعْبُدُونِ ﴾

"And I (Allah) created not the jinns and men except they should worship Me (Alone)." (V.51:56)

Allah also stated:

﴿ يَٰٓأَيُّهَا الَّذِينَ ءَامَنُوا اتَّقُوا اللَّهَ وَلْتَنظُرْ نَفْسٌ مَّا قَدَّمَتْ لِغَدٍ وَاتَّقُوا اللَّهَ إِنَّ اللَّهَ خَبِيرٌ بِمَا تَعْمَلُونَ ○ وَلَا تَكُونُوا كَالَّذِينَ نَسُوا اللَّهَ فَأَنسَىٰهُمْ أَنفُسَهُمْ أُوْلَٰئِكَ هُمُ الْفَٰسِقُونَ ○ لَا يَسْتَوِىٓ أَصْحَٰبُ النَّارِ وَأَصْحَٰبُ الْجَنَّةِ أَصْحَٰبُ الْجَنَّةِ هُمُ الْفَآئِزُونَ ﴾

"O you who believe! Fear Allah and keep your duty to Him. And let every person look to what he has sent forth for the morrow, and fear Allah. Verily, Allah is All-Aware of what you do. And be not like those who forgot Allah (i.e. became disobedient to Allah) and He caused them to forget their ownselves, (let them to forget to do righteous deeds). Those are the *Fâsiqûn* (rebellious, disobedient to Allah). Not equal are the dwellers of the Fire and the dwellers of the Paradise. It is the dwellers of Paradise that will be successful. (V. 59:18-20)

Allah also said:

﴿ فَمَن يَعْمَلْ مِثْقَالَ ذَرَّةٍ خَيْرًا يَرَهُ ○ وَمَن يَعْمَلْ مِثْقَالَ ذَرَّةٍ شَرًّا يَرَهُ ﴾

"So whosoever does good equal to the weight of an atom (or a small ant), shall see it. And whosoever does evil equal to the weight of an atom (or a small ant), shall see it." (V.99:7,8)

When the Muslim remembers these verses and other similar verses of the Glorious Qur'ân, he understands his aim in this worldly life and acquires knowledge about the true life of Hereafter which is certain to come. Therefore, he serves Allah devoutly and strives to gain His consent and kindness in this life and in the Hereafter. This will stimulate him to fulfil his religious duties sincerely, search for happiness in supplicating to Allah and gain tranquillity by continuous remembrance of Allah. Such a man is always good in deed and words. He gains praise and appreciation of other good men, and pays no heed to ungrateful envious men who deny religion and mock at pious men's efforts. He follows the way of the Messengers of Allah, and in whatever he does or says, he seeks nothing but the favour of Allah. Wherever he may work, he strives hard to increase production in order to serve Islâm and Muslims, knowing that Allah will reward him for his sincerity and good intention, and that his earnings by which he supports himself and his family will be blessed by Allah.

This manner of life secures honour and complete contentment for man. He can enjoy all legal pleasures without extravagance. He can have a wife and children who will serve Allah, add to the number of good Muslims and continue to carry out their father's mission after his death. A Muslim always thanks Allah for His favours and becomes more sincere to Him by devout obedience.

When a Muslim is afflicted with any disaster (fear, hunger, illness, ... etc), he knows well that Allah tests him,

101

therefore he should endure, be contented and thank Allah in all cases. In this way, Allah rewards him for his patience.

A Muslim leading his life with this high spirit and striving for the happy eternal life will gain happiness not even in this worldly life but also in the Hereafter.

Allah says:

﴿ تِلْكَ ٱلدَّارُ ٱلْأَخِرَةُ نَجْعَلُهَا لِلَّذِينَ لَا يُرِيدُونَ عُلُوًّا فِي ٱلْأَرْضِ وَلَا فَسَادًا وَٱلْعَٰقِبَةُ لِلْمُتَّقِينَ ﴾

"That home of the Hereafter (i.e. Paradise), We shall assign to those who rebel not against the truth with pride and oppression in the land nor do mischief by committing crimes. And the good end is for the *Muttaqûn*: [i.e. pious and righteous persons who fear Allah much (abstain from all kinds of sins and evil deeds which He has forbidden), and love Allah much (perform all kinds of good deeds which He has ordained)]." (V.28:83)

﴿ مَنْ عَمِلَ صَٰلِحًا مِّن ذَكَرٍ أَوْ أُنثَىٰ وَهُوَ مُؤْمِنٌ فَلَنُحْيِيَنَّهُۥ حَيَوٰةً طَيِّبَةً وَلَنَجْزِيَنَّهُمْ أَجْرَهُم بِأَحْسَنِ مَا كَانُوا۟ يَعْمَلُونَ ﴾

"Whoever works righteousness, whether male or female, while he (or she) is a true believer (of Islamic Monotheism) verily, to him We will give a good life (in this world with respect, contentment and lawful provision), and We shall pay them certainly a reward in proportion to the best of what they used to do (i.e. Paradise in the Hereafter)." (V.16:97)

The Prophet ﷺ said:

«عَجَبًا لِلْمُؤْمِنِ إِنَّ أَمْرَهُ كُلَّهُ لَهُ خَيْرٌ إِنْ أَصَابَتْهُ سَرَّاءُ شَكَرَ فَكَانَ خَيْرًا لَهُ، وَ إِنْ أَصَابَتْهُ ضَرَّاءُ صَبَرَ فَكَانَ خَيْرًا لَهُ»

"How fortunate is the believer! All his affairs are rewarding, if he is blessed with a favour, he thanks Allah and gains the reward of the thankful men, and if he is afflicted with a misfortune, he endures and gains the reward of the patient men."

All these evidences prove that Islâm is the only source of true conceptions, and the right criteria to distinguish truth from falsehood. All prevailing conceptions in the fields of sociology, economics, politics, education and other fields of knowledge should be revised and corrected according to the true principles of Islâm. It is impossible for any contrary conception to gain success, but it would rather impede progress and continue to be a source of misery and unhappiness to those who adopt it.

Chapter Five

Shedding Light on some
Erroneous Conceptions imputed to Islâm

The offenders against Islâm can be divided generally into two categories:- The first category contains those who claim to be Muslims, but they disobey Islâm, and commit deeds contrary to its principles. Among this category are:-

1. Those who pervert from the right faith and circumambulate tombs asking the dead for help, believing that dead pious men have the power to bring them benefits or prevent harm from them.

2. The slacker, broken up and loose person who rejects the Commandments of Allah and commits grave sins, or keeps intimacy with the enemies of Allah and follows their indecent mode of life.

3. Those who are weak in faith, neglect certain religious duties, and commit abominated vices like telling lies, breaking a promise and cheating. Although the sins committed by these people are not as grievous as idolatry, yet they offend Islâm by their abominable behaviour.

The second category, of those who offend against Islâm are the Orientalists, Christian Missionaries, Jews and other rancorous offenders of Islâm who follow them.

The widespread acceptability of Islâm and its magnanimous and characteristic traits upset these men. Islâm, being the Religion of Truth, is consistent with the innate nature of man. This characteristic trait of Islâm paves the way for a happy life for the Muslim, whereas every non-Muslim feels it inconsistent with his own creed, because it contradicts, in a way or another, the innate character of man.

Rancorous Orientalists and Missionaries invented lies against Islâm and Prophet Muhammad صلى الله عليه وسلم, tried to impute false accusations against the Prophet and tried to disgrace the Laws of Allah in order to alienate people from Islâm, but Allah always ruins their mechanism and they will never gain victory over Islâm, because they are struggling against the truth; the truth always overcomes and prevails over falsehood. Allah states in the Qur'ân:

﴿يُرِيدُونَ لِيُطْفِـُٔوا نُورَ ٱللَّهِ بِأَفْوَٰهِهِمْ وَٱللَّهُ مُتِمُّ نُورِهِۦ وَلَوْ كَرِهَ ٱلْكَٰفِرُونَ ۞ هُوَ ٱلَّذِىٓ أَرْسَلَ رَسُولَهُۥ بِٱلْهُدَىٰ وَدِينِ ٱلْحَقِّ لِيُظْهِرَهُۥ عَلَى ٱلدِّينِ كُلِّهِۦ وَلَوْ كَرِهَ ٱلْمُشْرِكُونَ﴾

"They intend to put out the Light of Allah (i.e. the Religion of Islam, this Qur'ân, and the Prophet Muhammad صلى الله عليه وسلم) with their mouths. But Allah will complete His Light even though the disbelievers hate (it). He it is Who has sent His Messenger (Muhammad صلى الله عليه وسلم) with guidance and the religion of truth (Islamic Monotheism) to make it victorious over all (other) religions even though the Mushrikûn (polytheists, pagans, idolaters, and disbelievers in the Oneness of Allah and in His Messenger Muhammad صلى الله عليه وسلم) hate (it)." (V.61:8,9)

The Sources of Islâm

Any wise man who wishes to acquire correct knowledge about Islâm should refer first to the Glorious Qur'ân and then to Prophetic traditions. Reliable books which contain authentic Prophetic traditions are *Sahih Al-Bukhâri, Sahih*

Muslim, Mowatta Imâm Malik, Musnad Ahmad Ibn Hanbal, Sunan Abû Dâwûd, Sunan An-Nasa'i, Sunan At-Tirmidhi, Sunan Ibn Mâjah and *Sunan Ad-Dârmi.* The book of *As-Seerah An-Nabawiyah* written by Ibn Hishâm contains the biography of Prophet Muhammad صلى الله عليه وسلم. Among the recommended books for one who wants to read about Islâm are: the book *Zâd Al-Ma'âd* by Ibn Al-Qaiyim, the works of Imam Ibn Taimiyah and the books of the reformer Muhammad bin Abdul Wahhab. Allah supported Islâm and Monotheism in the 12th century of *Hijra* through the reformer Muhammad bin Abdul Wahhab and prince Muhammad bin Sa'ud who uprooted idolatry and re-established the Monotheistic faith in the Arab Peninsula.

One who searches for the right knowledge about Islâm, should avoid reading books of Orientalists, Missionaries and other enemies of Islâm as they contain nothing but invented lies against Islâm, insults and abuses against Prophet Muhammad صلى الله عليه وسلم, his Companions and eminent *Imâm* of Islâm.

The Islâmic Schools of Thoughts

The basic ideology of all Muslims is Islâm, and in matters concerning their religion they refer to nothing save the Qur'ân and Prophetic traditions. The Islâmic schools of thoughts (like *Hanbalî, Mâlikî, Shâfa'i,* and *Hanafî*) are all basically based on Qur'ân and Prophetic traditions, but they may differ in some subsidiary questions of jurisprudence. Each one of these four *Imâm* taught his disciples his own methods and rules which he deduced from his studies of the Qur'ân and Prophetic traditions, but the four schools are all in agreement with the basis of Islâmic faith and law. However it is not obligatory for a Muslim to follow the conceptions of one of these schools, but he is commanded to follow the precepts of the Qur'ân and Prophetic traditions.

Sects that deviated from the Straight Path of Islâm

There are certain sects which assume unduly that they belong to Islâm, while they are flagrant disbelievers.

1. The first of these sects is the *Bâtiniyah* Sect which believes in incarnation and transmigration of souls and claim that the verses of the Qur'ân have a secret meaning which no one can know or derive except them. This disbelieving sect prefers the so-called hidden meaning of the Qur'ân, which they invent in accordance with their own desires to distort the obvious meaning elucidated by Prophet Muhammad صلى الله عليه وسلم himself.

This sect was primarily formed by a group of Jews, Magians and heretic Persians who joined hands to resist and impede the widespread of Islâm. They invented this misleading tenet to disperse Muslims and confuse their understanding of the Qur'ân. They affiliated themselves falsely with the Prophet and claimed unduly to be of his descendants. By these malicious and cunning methods, they succeeded in misleading a big number of ignorant common people.

2. The second disbelieving sect is *Quadyanism*. The impostor Ghulam Ahmad, who arrogated himself to prophethood, invented this misleading doctrine in India, and called the mobs there to believe in him. Ghulam Ahmad gave a false legal opinion that the religious duty of fighting against enemies of Islâm had been abrogated and called people to surrender and co-operate with the imperialist British authorities in India. By this method he gained the influence and financial support of the British authorities. Ghulam Ahmad strived hard to falsify and

destroy Islâm. He printed his books *Tasdiq Brâhîn Ahmadiyah*, *Tiryâq-ul-Qulûb* etc. and succeeded in misleading many groups in India. He died in 1908 and his deputy Nuruddin Hakim succeeded him. Even at present his descendants claim themselves "caliphs" of the founder of this sect.

3. The third disbelieving sect is the *Baha'iyah* which was formed in the 19th century by a Persian called Muhammad Alî Shirazi. This disbeliever first arrogated himself to be "the Mahdi," then pretended that God incarnated in him. He denied belief in Resurrection, Reckoning, Paradise and Hell-fire. Finally he denied that Muhammad صلى الله عليه وسلم is the last Prophet and rejected belief in the principle of Islâm.

After his death, his minister Baha replaced him and this disbelieving sect took its name from this minister's name.

Among the sects that deviated from the straight path of Islâm, although they claim to be Muslims is one big sect derived from *Shi'a*. The followers of this sect pretend to be Muslims i.e. they pray, fast and perform *Hajj*. They claim that Jibrael عليه السلام had commited dishonesty by conveying the Message (Revelation) to Prophet Muhammad صلى الله عليه وسلم while it was originally meant for 'Ali رضى الله عنه.

One of their big slanders is their claim that the Qur'ân had been tampered with, that there have been both additions to it and omissions from it.

They curse the best Muslims after Prophet Muhammad صلى الله عليه وسلم i.e. Abû Bakr and 'Umar رضى الله عنهما. They also curse 'Aisha, *Umm-ul-Mu'minîn* (the Mother of the Believers) رضى الله عنها.

The members of this sect seek help from 'Ali رضى الله عنه and from his sons and call them for assistance.

They call themselves *Shi'a* i.e. *Shi'at-al-Bait* (the adherents of the descendants of the House of Prophet Muhammad صلى الله عليه وسلم).

It should be known that 'Ali رضى الله عنه and his sons were innocent from what the *Shi'a* claim, because they considered them as partners to Allah. They lie therein and perverted the Speech of Allah, the All-Mighty.

The Muslims throughout the world should know that these sects and all other enemies of Islâm co-operate and strive hard to destroy Islâm. The best guide for the Muslim is the Qur'ân and Prophetic traditions. A true Muslim pondering on the Qur'ân and Prophetic traditions will never be mislead and will attain eternal bliss and happiness in the Hereafter.

A Call for Salvation

This is a call to every wise person who wants to deliver himself from the torment of Hell-fire in the Hereafter, as well as the torment of the grave after death.

Dear Readers

Hurry up to rescue yourself and gain salvation. Believe that Allah is your God and that there is no god save Allah and believe that Muhammad صلى الله عليه وسلم is His Messenger. Embrace Islâm, perform prayer, pay the *Zakât*, perform pilgrimage to the House of Allah if you have the means to do so. Declare openly that you are a Muslim to Allah.

I swear by Allah that there is no way for deliverance and salvation save Islâm, I swear by Allah Who is the only God that the religion of Islâm is the Religion of Truth, and that Allah will accept no other religion from anybody.

I call Allah, His angels, and all His creation as witnesses to my testimony that there is no god save Allah and that Muhammad صلى الله عليه وسلم is the Messenger of Allah, and that Islâm is the true religion.

I invoke Allah to bless me and make me die while being a true Muslim so that I may dwell in Paradise in companionship with our honest Prophet Muhammad صلى الله عليه وسلم and all the Prophets of Allah.

May Allah make this book useful for all those who read it.

May the blessings and peace of Allah be upon our Prophet Muhammad and his Companions.

All praise is to Allah, the Lord of all worlds.

الصف التصويري والإخراج ـ *الفرقان* المملكة العربية السعودية الرياض ١١٤٧٥
ص.ب ٢١٤٤١ ـ هاتــف ٤٠٤٣٧٣٢ ـ ٤٠٢٦٦٧٤ فاكـس ٤٠٤٣٧٨٧